Eva Hesmondhalgh
238 Sanderstead Rd,
South Croydon,
Surrey,
CR2 0AJ.
0181 657-6251

Thirteensomething

Thirteensomething

Written and illustrated by Jane Goldman

Piccadilly Press . London

This book is dedicated with love and kisses to the utterly
wonderful Jonathan and Betty

And also to . . .
My fabulous family: Amanda and Stuart (world's best
parents), Kinny, Bunker and Anny.

Oh yeah and . . .
Two totally brilliant friends, Jacqui and Chrissy, who helped
me enormously with this book, and some other totally brilliant
friends who didn't but deserve a mention anyway: Monica,
Max, Rowland, Toula and Juliette.

And . . .
My tremendous in-laws – especially Maureen, Amanda, Simon
and Liza for their friendship and support.

And finally . . .
To James – the coolest Thirteensomething person I know.

Phototypset by Creative Text Ltd., London
Printed and bound by Progressive Printing (UK) Ltd., Leigh-on-Sea, Essex.
for the Publishers, Piccadilly Press Ltd. 5 Castle Road, London NW1 8PR
Reprinted 1994, 1995

A catalogue record for this book is available from the British Library.

ISBN 1 85340 246 X (trade paperback)
ISBN 1 85340 222 2 (hardback)

Jane Goldman was born in 1970. She lives in North London with her
husband and small daughter. She worked for a number of years for *Just
17*, and is now a freelance journalist and writer. This is her first book.

Contents

Chapter One

SCHOOL

DO WE *REALLY* HAVE TO DO THIS?

Life is full of surprises. Take going to school, for instance. There you are, a happy toddler, minding your own business, enjoying long, joyous days creating your own entertainment and learning new things for yourself (i.e. chocolate tastes nice, crayons and worms don't, spreading nappy cream on the carpet makes Mum turn a funny red colour and shout a lot etc.) and then - bang! - for no apparent reason you begin a prison sentence that's going to last until you're at least 16. Once you figure out that this is something that happens to everybody and not just a particularly harsh punishment for the nappy cream incident, you do your best to get into the swing of things. "Okay," you figure, "this isn't too bad. I can deal with this. I can easily cope with another decade or so of painting pictures, sticking wool to egg cartons, pouring water through funnels and getting stories read to me.

No problemo." Then they start landing you with
enchanting concepts like maths, joined-up writing and
homework and it dawns on you that this isn't going to
be as easy as you'd originally imagined. Once you hit
eleven, the full horror of your plight has probably sunk
in. You no longer wish to take this lying down, but you
don't appear to have any choice in the matter. To make
things worse, adults helpfully insist on telling you to
enjoy it, because these are the best years of your life.
"You mean to say it gets worse?" you wonder miserably,
as you try desparately to suss out what you did to
deserve all this. In my opionion, adults who suggest
that life goes downhill after school deserve to be sent
back for another 11 years of it, not least to jog their
memories because they've obviously forgotten just how
hard it can be. Although adult life certainly does mean
loads of extra stuff to worry about, it's generally a far, far
better deal all round. Just think about it - you have the
freedom to do what you want, see who you want, *be* who
you want. You still have to work hard every day, but
hopefully you get to work at doing something you like,
and even if you don't like it, you get paid for it, and you
get to drink coffee while you're doing it.
  Feeling optimistic about the future is great, but it's
surprisingly little help when you're feeling really
grimabout the present. There are bound to be times
(especially when faced with an afternoon of double
geography) when you've wished you didn't have to

bother with school at all. Looking on the positive side, there are a lot of good things about going to school even when you're not enjoying it. School gets you acquainted with general skills that'll come in handy in later life - like doing stuff you hate on a day-to-day basis, dealing with loathsome people and taking everything in your stride. If you didn't go to school, real life would come as a horrible shock. It also develops your memory, gives you a chance to find out what interests you and teaches you useful basic things you'll need in life like reading, writing and doing stuff with numbers. Makes some kind of sense, doesn't it?

In truth, we're all prepared to take on board the fact that we have to go to school, and when we wonder "Why on earth do we have to do this?" it's usually more specific things we have in mind. We all know, for instance, that there is unlikely to come a day in our adult life when we say "Phew, that was a close one, thank goodness I knew the Pythagoras theorem!" You are also unlikely to find much use for knowledge of the density of water, the capital of Assyria or the hierarchy of the Feudal System. The point is, you wonder exactly why on earth you have to learn oodles and oodles of information you are never going to be able to put to any use. Try asking a teacher or your parents and you'll probably be told that you need to know these things in order to pass exams, and you need to pass exams in order to get a good job or go to university (and then get a good job). Fair enough, one supposes, but little comfort when you're slogging through a lesson so tedious that you wonder if you'll die of boredom before you make it to adulthood anyway. It's always useful to have some little thought with which to comfort yourself in your hour of misery, some little reason why all this torment is going to be worthwhile. Can't think of any? Don't fret: use some of these ...

The very useful guide to things to keep in mind in order to survive painfully dull lessons

English Literature

The good thing about English Literature lessons is that you often get given good, interesting books to read. The bad thing about them is that you are forced to study and pick them to bits until they become boring beyond belief. The key to surviving these horrors is to enjoy the knowledge that if you remember a few snippets from the books you're being forced to read (especially the "classics"), you'll be able to impress people by appearing tremendously clever and well-read, even if you choose to read only comics and the backs of cereal packets for the rest of your life.

English Language

If you think you're never going to need to understand past participles and suchlike once you're out in the real world, you're absolutely right. Looking on the bright side, though, the better the grasp you have of the English language, the more articulate and literate you'll be. In real terms, this means you'll be able to win arguments, influence people's ways of thinking, write really great letters and generally get your own way more often - doesn't sound too bad, eh?

Science

Some of the things you learn in science may truly come in handy, such as how your body works, how plants grow and why lighting a match during a gas leak is a really crap idea. Absorb the stuff that can be put to any practical use later on, and regard the rest - the endless tables and formulas - as a good workout for your brain which, like any other part of your body, needs its exercise.

Languages

Travelling is one of life's great joys, and being able to speak the local language increases the pleasure of travel even more. Of course, you may feel that learning French or German at school is all very well, but won't do you much good if you're really yearning to visit Greece, Russia, Mexico, Outer Mongolia etc. In fact, the more you learn about the structure of a language (*any* language), the easier it'll be for you to pick up the language of your choice when you come to learn it. It can still be mighty frustrating, however, when instead of learning phrases that might come in handy, such as "Could you please direct me to the nearest reasonably priced hotel, please?", you're being taught how to say things like "The monkey has taken my aunt's hat." The best way to get through lessons like these is to keep yourself amused by working out ways that you'll be able to put all this to good use - for instance, you only need lure your auntie to a safari park in France, trick her into wearing a special hat you've cunningly decorated with bananas, and voilà - you've got a primo opportunity to impress everyone with your grasp of the lingo.

Geography, History, Political Studies etc.

The wonderful thing about the information in these
lessons is that they are the key to appearing intelligent
in later life. In truth, intelligence has very little to do
with storing information, but people tend to judge your
brain-power by whether you know more pieces of
useless information than them, and this is just the kind
of stuff that really impresses. Appearing intelligent has
all sorts of benefits, including intimidating people you
don't like, winning respect from your friends and
acquiring instant sex-appeal (yes, being clever is an
enormous turn-on). Look on these lessons as golden
opportunities to stuff your memory banks: absorb as
much as you can, then sit back and enjoy daydreams of a
future in which you impress all your friends at dinner
parties by beating them spectacularly at Trivial Pursuit,
or appear on TV quiz shows and win huge amounts of
money.

Maths

I can't pretend that all of the stuff you learn in maths is
going to come in handy, *literally* - indeed, once you've
left school, the chances of you ever having to work out a
fraction are low, to say the least (and so are the chances

THIRTEENSOMETHING

of you ever having to work out the chances of something happening - I mean, you didn't mind that I just said "low" instead of something like "one in 57", did you?). A basic understanding of numbers, however, is a nice thing to have. Not only does it add to your intelligent image (see above) but being able to do things like add, subtract, multiply, divide and work out percentages (especially in your head rather than on paper) enables you to shine in lots of situations involving money. You can wow prospective employers by grumbling at how low the wage they've offered you will be once it's been taxed, showoff to current employers by demanding pay-rises in line with inflation, intimidate people who try to cheat you out of money, be a whizz at gambling, and generally confuse and impress everyone by doing lots of complicated mathematics in front of them for no apparent reason.

Physical Education And Sports

Even in small measures, physical exertion improves your general health, helps prevent you from getting fat and exercises your heart, so improving your chances of living longer - a pretty good deal all told, unless, of course, you're particularly keen on the idea of being flabby, ill or dead, in which case I can't help you.

Computer Studies

When this lesson drags, just remember: the more you know about computers, the more you'll be able to impress and intimidate virtually everyone over the age of 26. They may be older, wiser and have all the money, but even the ones who understand computers still get a bit spooked by people who grew up with them. Make no mistake, computer literacy is going to be one of your most powerful weapons when it comes to getting ahead, and even if you don't plan to touch another computer once you leave school, every moment you spend paying attention now will give you a very real edge.

Art, Technical Drawing And Craft

What should you bear in mind when you get bored and frustrated during art and craft lessons? Just be thankful it's not maths, I guess.

TEACHERS

There are eight basic breeds of teacher. Here's how to
identify and deal with them ...

Mr. Stroppy

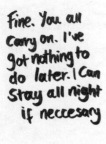

Good points: Not known.

Bad points: Everything.

Favourite saying: "Get out!"

How to get on his good side: Leave the school.

How to get on his bad side: Breathe.

Warning: Will never, ever leave.

Mr. Unbelievably Nice

Good points: Really good fun.

Bad points: Barking mad.

Favourite saying: "Let's have today's lesson outside!"

How to get on his good side: Join in the fun.

How to get on his bad side: Point out that it's raining when he says "Let's have today's lesson outside!" or mention the National Curriculum.

Warning: Likely to get the sack, sharpish.

THIRTEENSOMETHING

Ms. Hysterical

Good points: Gullible.

Bad points: Cries a lot.

Favourite saying: "You'll all be sorry when I'm dead!"

How to get on her good side: Encourage your classmates to behave well.

How to get on her bad side: Encourage all your classmates to make loud continuous humming noises with their mouths closed so she can't tell where it's coming from.

Warning: Likely to have nervous breakdown, possibly in class.

I'm not going to ask you all to be quiet again! Okay, I am going to ask you again... BE QUIET!!! Please? Oh please do be quiet now... Waaaah!

Ms. Bouncy

Good points: Cheerful and enthusiastic.

Bad points: Alarmingly cheerful and enthusiastic.

Favourite saying: "Everybody happy?!"

How to get on her good side: Breathe.

How to get on her bad side: Set fire to her car and murder her family.

Warning: Could drive you insane.

Wow! Today we're going to do algebra! My favourite!

Ms. Mad

Good points: On another planet most of the time.

Bad points: Returns to planet Earth just when you've done something wrong.

Favourite saying:"Now, where was I?"

How to get on her good side: Humour her.

How to get on her bad side: Make it too obvious that you're humouring her.

Warning: Unpredictable.

HaHaHa...
NoHoHoHo...
Hooo! oh
excuse me, but
I just find
Shakespeare
so funny!
HaHaHa!

Ms. Bossy

Good points: Is exceptionally nice to favourites.

Bad points: Is exceptionally unpleasant to everyone else.

Favourite sayings: "Because I say so", "Life's not fair" and "You're not the only pebble on the beach".

How to get on her good side: Keep your head down, stay quiet, fit in.

How to get on her bad side: Fail to do the above.

Warning: Can somehow see exactly what you're doing when her back is turned.

If nobody is going to own up, you can *all* stay behind...

Mr. Ancient

Good points: Short memory, sluggish, much hilarity to be had when he forgets what age group he is teaching and asks if anyone needs to use the toilet.

Bad points: Grumpy, especially when he's just woken up halfway through a lesson.

Favourite saying: "Show respect to your elders!"

How to get on his good side: Show respect.

How to get on his bad side: Bellow "Wakey wakey, Grandpa!" in his ear.

Warning: Can sense what you're doing even when asleep. Prone to sudden displays of perfect memory and ability to speak clearly (especially when reporting you to the head teacher).

In my day we had to write our homework on a slate, by candle-light and we never had problems with handing it in on time

Mr. Psycho

Good points: Highly intelligent, interesting.

Bad points: Terrifying.

Favourite saying: "Just think about it ..."

How to get on his good side: Express interest in the enormous nuclear reactor he is building behind the bike shed.

How to get on his bad side: Alert the authorities to the above.

Warning: Will give you nightmares.

... which clearly proves that Earth is going to be obliterated by a large meteor, probably within your lifetimes. Any questions?

ATTACK OF THE KILLER Bs!

School may not be a barrel of fun all the time (or indeed any of the time) but you can guarantee that it'll be a full-blown nightmare if you find yourself tangled up with the following stressworthy and serious situations ...

Bullying

Being bullied is one of the most hideous experiences that can happen to you in school. The physical pain of getting attacked, the humiliation of verbal abuse and the fear of what the bully is going to do next are nasty enough things to have to cope with, but they're not the end of the story. People who are bullied usually also feel that they have somehow failed, and that there is something wrong with them just because they are disliked by a bully. All these feelings add up to a hateful situation which gets harder and harder to deal with the longer it goes on. The quickest, most sure-fire way of putting a stop to bullying is to report it to a teacher, or tell your parents so that they can do it for you, but it's surprising how many victims are reluctant to do this for one reason or another. Should you tell on a bully? The answer is very straightforward: *of course* you should. If you let a bully get away with what they're doing, you are helping and protecting them at your own expense.

The so-called "rules of the playground" (an unwritten code of practice which says that it's not on to involve adults in your business) is a load of old rubbish that was made up by bullies in the first place to protect themselves. You are not being wet, wimpy or childish by involving an adult - on the contrary, reporting a bully is the act of someone who is brave, strong and mature.

You can also be sure that the bully is picking on someone else too - so you won't just be helping yourself, but someone else who isn't as strong-willed as you. The other fear that puts people off reporting that they're being bullied is the fear that their parents will think they have "failed" at being popular at school. It's important to remember that bullying rarely has anything to do with popularity, and it's the bully who has a problem getting along with people, not the victim. Besides, your parents are far more concerned about your welfare than anything else. It's really not worth letting *any* fear stand in your way (including the fear of the bully getting nastier if you report him or her), because as anyone who has ever told on a bully can tell you, the over-riding feeling once you've done the deed is pure relief. If you really can't bring yourself to tell on the bully, there are options you could try for dealing with the situation yourself. They may work or they may not. The first thing worth trying is to ignore the bully. It just might do the trick, especially if the bullying is of the verbal teasing variety, because a bully will often lose interest in their little game when they stop getting a response from their victim. The other course of action that's worth a shot is standing up to the bully, as he or she might decide that bullying you is too much trouble if you're going to fight back. If neither of these efforts make any difference, then it's time to seriously reconsider telling an adult. These days, in the light of several suicides due to bullying, schools take it all very seriously indeed, so you should always be guaranteed swift action.

Putting a stop to bullying should be *everybody's* responsibility, not just the victim's. If you see someone else being bullied, or know that it's going on, behave as you'd want others to behave if you were the victim - step in and stand up for them, or tell an adult what's going on. If you're friends with a bully, talk to them about why they bully others, and try to let them know that you don't approve, even if you're scared of them. The main thing to remember is that no one has a right to make anyone else's life a misery.

Bunking Off

Skipping school is not a great idea in any circumstance. If you do it because you're getting bullied, have no friends or are having trouble with school work, you're just running away from the problem and creating a new one for yourself in the process - the only way to make a problem go away is to deal with it directly. If you do it just for the hell of it, or just because you're bored at school, it's still a pretty pointless exercise in itself, regardless of parental fury, getting in trouble at school and falling behind in lessons.

There's a rather brilliant film that was made back in the eighties by the director John Hughes, called *Ferris Bueller's Day Off* (if you haven't seen it, rent it on video - it's great) in which a boy, his girlfriend and his best mate skip school and spend a day out in the big city. They go to a baseball game, have lunch in a posh restaurant and visit an art gallery. It's all enormously entertaining, but hold on, just who are the Hollywood film-makers kidding? The reality of bunking off school is that you end up doing the most dull, mundane things - hanging around shopping centres, mooching about the house and generally doing nothing of any real entertainment value at all, and all the while worrying about being spotted by an adult and caught out. If kids really played truant in order to go to art galleries, I'm sure no one would be quite as bothered about the whole affair, but that's really not the case, is it? If you think about it, bunking off in order to do something that is probably equally as dull as going to school (if not duller), simply because it's not as much effort, is really not worth the trouble it can get you into.

21

Being Incredibly Unpopular

There's nothing more miserable than having no friends at school. You dread going in, you can't tell anyone about your problem, and you feel like a failure. This is a common situation for people who move to new schools, especially if you're the only new person in a class. The first thing to remember in those cases is that you're not necessarily unpopular - it can take time to make friends, and often all you need is a bit of patience. If you feel like you've waited long enough and done your best already, or you're not new in the school at all but you're short of pals anyway, then it's possible that it's still not your fault at all. It's more likely that the people you're trying to make friends with are being snotty and unreceptive (if they're the most popular people in the class, it's probably a simple case of being too big for their boots because of their popularity), in which case you were on to a loser from the beginning.

If you suspect this is what's up, try befriending the quieter, less "popular" people instead - they're probably much nicer anyway. Still think you've got a problem? To help solve it, you should try to look a little closer at yourself, in order to find out what is stopping people from being friends with you. Ask yourself these questions:

★ *Have you tried to make friends?*

Sometimes it's just a simple matter of making the first move yourself. If people are happily settled with their own friends, they may not feel like making the effort to befriend anyone else, but they'll probably be thrilled and flattered if you show an interest in being friends with them. Unfortunately, being very quiet and shy and keeping yourself to yourself can often be misinterpreted as "stuck-up" or snotty behaviour - if you haven't made an effort to get chatting, people could assume that you're not interested in getting to know them.

★ *Are you loud or boastful?*

Showing off, making incessant jokes and generally doing things that demand attention rarely wins any friends. It not only gives the impression that you're desperate, but it's also unattractive behaviour, and likely to put people off wanting to get to know you better, because you're embarrassing. Being yourself is always the best bet.

★ *Do you talk about people behind their backs?*

Even if you think that bitching about unpopular people will get others on your side, all it really does is make you appear mean-spirited and untrustworthy. It's a hugely off-putting habit, so don't do it!

★ *Are you ultra-nice?*

Being friendly wins points, but being crawly is the kiss of death. If you constantly agree with things people say, regularly compliment them on their clothes, talents etc, stand close by them even when you're not involved in their conversation or buy them presents, you are being crawly, and it's very off-putting. Most people want friends who are happy, balanced and behave normally. This kind of grovelling says quite the opposite about you, and will repel just about anyone, except perhaps people who are looking for a doormat-type friend to boss around and walk all over. You may feel that *any* friendship is better than none at all, but a friendship that is unbalanced, where one person is just "using" the other and doesn't respect them, is a horrible thing to be involved in.

★ *Do you dress differently to others?*

Sadly, many young people are very freaked-out by others who don't conform. Whether it's because of your religion, because you're not into fashion, or simply because you like to be individual, just the fact that you stand out can put people off you. Psychologists say that it's because dressing differently sends a silent message to your classmates that you don't like the way they dress (hence you dress differently). However, you should never need to change the way you look to suit others - just make an extra effort to get talking to people, show them that you like *them* the way *they* are, and once they've got to know your personality, they'll be bound to forget all about how you look.

If you think any of these reasons might apply to your difficulty in making friends, you should remember that there is nothing terrible about any of them. The great thing is that if you can pinpoint the cause of a problem, you're halfway towards solving it, and it's never too late to make a fresh start by either making more effort or toning things down a bit. Making the first move to get to know people can be scary, especially if you tend to be shy, but it's not really as hard as all that: just smile a lot, be friendly and pleasant, ask people lots of questions about themselves (people love talking about themselves!), and listen carefully to what they have to say to you. Do all these things, and you'll find that you'll be having friendly chats.

HOMEWORK

Homework is just one of life's necessary evils. Everyone has their own way of organising their personal timetable to get homework done, but it basically breaks down to two options.

The first goes like this:

4.30 p.m.   Arrive home.

4.32 p.m.   Have a quick snack, set video to record TV programmes that you might want to watch sometime.

4.42 p.m.   Do homework.

5.52 p.m.   Do everything else.

The second goes like this:

4.30 p.m.	Arrive home. Have a quick snack.
4.42 p.m.	Watch TV until there's nothing on worth watching.
6.30 p.m.	Long chat on phone with friend you last saw a couple of hours ago.
7.00 p.m.	Dinner.
7.30 p.m.	Read TV guide to find out what's on later. Get distracted by faintly interesting article.
7.40 p.m.	Twiddle thumbs. Wonder what fave pop star is doing right now.
7.45 p.m.	Have argument with parents about not having done homework yet.
8.00 p.m.	Start homework.
8.15 p.m.	Stop for quick snack.
8.30 p.m.	Stop for "quick" computer game.
9.30 p.m.	Try to finish homework. Fail.

9.45 p.m.	Look at watch. Complain about how you never get to do anything interesting in the evenings.
9.50 p.m.	Try to finish homework, fall asleep with head on open book.1.00 a.m.Wake up with cricked neck.
1.02 a.m.	Go to bed. Desperately try to think of excuses for not having done homework. Fail. Worry.
4.00 a.m.	Wake up after nightmare where giant scorpion with the head of your teacher chases you and you're not wearing any clothes and everyone's laughing at you.
7.30 a.m.	Wonder if alarm clock has gone off early by mistake. Discover to your dismay that it hasn't.
7.35 a.m.	Panic some more about thinking up excuses whilst brushing teeth, getting dressed, propping eye-lids open with toothpicks etc.

Both methods have their distinct advantages and drawbacks. The first offers plenty of free time, but takes a certain amount of will-power. The second offers the chance to eat a lot and sample a wide variety of television programmes, but results in exhaustion, bad grades and stress. The choice is yours.

Chapter Two

BOYS AND GIRLS

BEYOND LUMPS, BUMPS AND DANGLY BITS

Here's an extensive list of the things that fascinate - and exasperate - boys and girls about the other ...

BOYS GET MYSTIFIED WHEN GIRLS ...	GIRLS GET MYSTIFIED WHEN BOYS ...
... Have a "best friend"	... Scorn the idea of a "best friend" and insist that they only have "mates"
... Get extremely upset if their best friend gets a new best friend	... Still get extremely upset if their favourite "mate" goes off with someone else

... Order "just a salad" at restaurants then pinch food off everyone else

... Appear to be under the impression that chips count as a nutritious vegetable

...Can tolerate having a friend who's notorious for her loud giggle

...Can tolerate having a friend who's notorious for farting all the time.

... Cry in films and enjoy it thoroughly

... Cry in films and pretend that they don't

THIRTEENSOMETHING

... Go to the loo in pairs and spend hours there chatting and putting on make-up

... Never go to the loo at all, or if they do, come out again right away without stopping to chat

... Always remember people's birthdays

... Never remember people's birthdays, or any other dates

... Dance together in a big circle (pile of handbags optional)

... Dance very well on their own but seem to think that dancing with a girl has to mean shuffling round in a circle to a Michael Bolton record whilst dribbling in their partner's ear

... Always notice when someone is wearing something new or has a hair cut, no matter how tiny the change

... Fail to notice what anyone is wearing to the point where you could probably meet them in a Sumo - Wrestler's nappy with a bucket on your head without them batting an eyelid

33

...Borrow their boyfriend's jumper, and tell as many people as possible who who it belongs to

...Brag to their mates about having a girlfriend but won't introduce her to them

...Insist on taking sweatshirts
or cardigans when they go
out in hot weather, then
tie them round their waists
the whole time

...Insist on wearing
summer clothes
in freezing
weather, then
staunchly refuse to
admit to being cold

...Insist on watching scary
films on video, then spend
quite large amounts of time
looking at the back of a
cushion

...Insist on watching
scary films
on video, refuse to
hide behind a cushion
for the sake of
bravado, then have
nightmares for a week

....Watch soap operas, then
discuss them at great length
with friends

...Claim not to watch
soaps but always
mysteriously know
what's happening in
all of them

... Fill up their shelves with
bits and bobs like china
animals and tiny notebooks

... Cultivate exotic
fungi and bacteria
amongst the
highly toxic mounds
of old clothing and
food under their beds

... Worry endlessly about the size of their bosoms

... Worry endlessly about the size of their willies

... Enjoy singing loudly and tunelessly with their friends in public

... Seem compelled to make "Pcchhhh pcchhh eeeooow pccchhh" noises while playing any arcade game that involves shooting things

...Watch videos in groups and rewind the bit where the bloke's shirt comes off

...Watch videos in groups and rewind the bit where the bloke's *head* comes off

... Write long letters to boys they've had holiday romances with

... Never get round to writing to girls they've had holiday romances with

... Write long letters to agony aunts when the boys they've had holiday romances with don't write

... Write long letters to agony aunts when the girls they forgot to write to refuse to speak to them the next year.

... Insist on meeting boys somewhere public on dates in case someone they know passes and sees them

... Insist on meeting girls somewhere discreet on dates in case someone they know passes by and sees them

THIRTEENSOMETHING

...Read stuff that boys consider to be "trash", girls' magazines, mail-order catalogues and adult novels where everybody goes shopping and has sex a lot

...Secretly read the the same things, but for *truly* trashy reasons, like the spicy problem-page letters, the mags, the undie and swimsuit pages in catalogues and the rude bits in novels

... Go to school with appalling illnesses because they can't bear to miss out on seeing their friends

... Stay at home at the merest sign of a runny nose and expect their mums to tuck them up in bed with a plate of Marmite soldiers (crusts cut off)

There's no doubt about it, the differences between the sexes run far deeper than the physical stuff. It's about now that you're probably beginning to notice all the other things - the funny behaviour, strange rituals and curious ways - which make the opposite sex such a mystery... And before you know it, the gender gap has widened into a whacking great chasm. The quirks of the opposite sex are sometimes charming, often annoying and always puzzling.

SO IF THIS IS LOVE ... WHEN DO WE GET TO THE EXCITING BIT?

When you were a kid, it seemed like all the TV programmes, films, books and magazines you saw were primarily concerned with good guys, bad guys and fluffy animals that could talk and/or sing. Now all of a sudden you're being bombarded with riveting fictional accounts of teenage *lurve* instead. This is largely okay, but it's sometimes baffling and depressing, because in the weird world of fiction, every romance is filled with intrigue, passion and earth-shattering events. Compare these sizzling dramas with real life, and the excitement score looks something like: fiction - ten, reality - nil. This will probably lead you to deduce the following: a) your life is terminally dull, b) everyone else's is incredibly interesting, and c) you might as well just forget the whole business of romance and apply immediately to become a nun/monk. Hopefully you haven't bought a stamp for your application yet, because the good news is that you're wrong. I'll show you why. Okay, now firstly, here's a brief account of a real - life teenage romance:

A boy called James decides he quite fancies a girl called Katie but doesn't bother to do anything about it. Two months later he wishes he had because she starts going

out with Steve from 5b. Another two months passes and
James sees Steve from 5b snogging Hayley from 5b after
school, so he decides to ask Katie out at last. It turns
out that Katie stopped seeing Steve from 5b ages ago, so
she's really pleased and they go on a date. It's quite nice.
They go on a few more until they discover that they
have very little in common and the whole thing
gradually dwindles off. The end.

That's real life for you, in all its glory. Gripping stuff,
eh? Well no, it isn't really. That's why the people who
write stories and TV shows and movies cook up fictional
accounts of love that are exciting, action-packed ... And
totally removed from real life. They may *seem* real, but
they're just make-believe, written by clever people
whose job it is to invent thrilling stuff for
entertainment purposes. Even when they get their ideas
from real life, you can bet that they've twisted and
embellished reality beyond all recognition. I'll show you
exactly what I mean. Here's their story as it might be
told by various craftsmen of the media:

The Photo-Love Story

Katie and James have been next-door neighbours for
years and years and although James has always fancied
Katie, Katie is more interested in hunky Steve from 5b.

She's overjoyed when Steve asks her out, but later discovers that he's two-timing her with Hayley from 5b. Dejected, she turns to faithful old James for comfort ... and suddenly realises that she fancied him all along!

The Magazine Short Story

Katie really fancies James, a mysterious boy who dresses in strange clothes whom she often speaks to in the hall at school. When she gets dumped by her boyfriend, Steve from 5b, she looks for James, but can't find him anywhere. She describes him to her teacher, who goes very pale and reveals that there was a boy called James who went to the school 30 years ago and died in a freak accident when he fell over in the hall and banged his head on a locker.

The Australian Soap Opera

James is dating Katie, who is new to the neighbourhood, and is devastated when he spots her snogging Steve from 5b. When he confronts her, she runs off in a huff. He finds her in the local cafe and apologises, but she doesn't seem to understand what he's on about. Steve from 5b walks in demanding to know why James is bothering his new girlfriend, Hayley.

Katie walks in and explains that Hayley is her identical twin. They all make up and go on a lovely double date.

The British Kids, TV Drama

James and Katie are dating, but nasty Steve from 5b is jealous. He spray-paints *James Woz 'Ere* on the classroom wall, getting James suspended for a month and making Katie's parents refuse to let her see him any more. Katie dates Steve instead, until he accidentally lets slip that he set James up. Katie apologises to James for not believing he was innocent, but he reveals that he is now seeing Hayley, who stood by him all along.

The American Teenage Novel

Katie is a rich teenage tennis champion who starts going out with scruffy James, the new kid in town whose dad works at the local garage. Her snooty ex-boyfriend Steve gets together with bitchy Hayley, Katie's arch - rival from the tennis club, to find some dirt on James and discovers that James's dad is actually an FBI man working undercover on a top secret investigation.

The Hollywood Movie

Katie (played by Winona Ryder) and James (played by Keanu Reeves) are madly in love, despite the presence of Steve from 5b (played by Kevin Costner pretending to be a teenager) who is constantly trying to split them up. Everything is wonderful until James discovers he has a terminal illness. Steve and James become friends and James makes Steve promise to look after Katie when he's gone. They all cry a lot to a rousing soundtrack sung by Whitney Houston.

Anyway, you get the picture - it's all a load of twaddle. The important thing is to enjoy the stuff you watch and read as pure entertainment, but remember: that's all it is.

THE DATING GAME

Dating is a funny old thing. It can be such enormous fun that you won't know what hit you, or it can be the most fraught, nerve-racking, embarrassing, unpleasant experience ever invented. The secret, by and large, is just to relax and enjoy it - after all, that's what it's supposed to be all about. The way to ensure that your date is a successful one (by which I mean any date that doesn't end with you locking yourself in your room and swearing you'll never do it again) is to avoid all the obvious pitfalls. "Good" dates don't usually happen by accident, and nor do bad ones. It's not just about chemistry between two people, because *everyone* is capable of having good dates and bad dates. Perhaps the easiest way of making a date go well is to avoid all the common pitfalls that can lead to disaster. The way I see it, if you can identify - and leave out - all the ingredients for a nightmare date, you'll be all set up for a good one. So here they are ...

Your handy checklist

Before you leave ...

❑ Get into a really frantic frame of mind. Nothing is guaranteed to spoil a date better than arriving in a state of near hysteria.

❑ Don't plan what to wear ahead of time: just get all your clothes out of your wardrobe and try on as many different things as possible. For optimum effectiveness your room should be fairly messy to start with, and the heating should be turned up to maximum to ensure that you get hot and sweaty while you're trying things on. It will be totally impossible to choose what to wear and you'll end up feeling really tired and horrible.

❑ Settle for something you feel uncomfortable in - possibly something that doesn't fit very well or something you've never worn before.

❑ Try as many hairstyles as possible, ideally when you only have a few minutes left. Handle your hair a great deal in the process so that it becomes lank and greasy.

❑ Totally avoid doing any homework before you leave, especially if it's due in the next day, and encourage your parents to comment on this.

❑ Have an argument with your parents regarding this or any other subject - it will contribute greatly to your bad mood.

❑ Be sure to squeeze any spots you have to make them more noticeable.

❏ Remember that this is the ideal time to try any cosmetic procedure for the first time, especially those which may produce unexpected blotchiness, i.e. plucking your eyebrows, applying aftershave.

❏ Tell yourself how unattractive you look.

Getting there ...

❏ Don't leave on time - try to be either very, very early, or preposterously late.

❏ If you're getting a lift from a parent, leave it until you're halfway there to tell them that you don't want anyone to see them dropping you off because it's embarrassing.

❏ If this fails to provoke an argument, try listing the reasons why they are such an embarrassment.

❏ If you have chosen to use public transport, ensure that you are totally unaware of the timetables so that you can miss the first bus or train and then be left wondering when the next one is coming.

Arriving ...

❏ The ideal location for your nightmare date is somewhere that a) a lot of other people arrange to meet each other so that it's crowded and difficult to find anyone and b) plenty of people you know are likely to be around to be a nuisance generally.

❏ If you are the first to arrive, pass the time by working yourself into a frenzy thinking about your hair, clothes, spots, homework and the possibility of being stood up.

When your date arrives ...

❏ Ideally, neither of you should have given any thought to what you want to do, enabling you to have the classic nightmare date conversation:

❏ Ask your date what they want to do.

❏ When they say
"I don't know, what do *you* want to do?", always reply
"I don't know, what do *you* want to do?"

❏ Repeat. If you get bored, try "I don't know, I asked you first" or "No, you decide" for variety.

THIRTEENSOMETHING

Once the date is underway ...

❏ If you're aiming for a true nightmare date, beware of activities like bowling, ice or roller-skating, seeing a film or visiting a games arcade - they make life much too easy by providing you with something to do and talk about afterwards.

❏ If you are going to the cinema, be sure that neither of you have any idea what is on or what you wish to see, so that you can have another really dull conversation following the same pattern as your previous conversation, and for goodness' sake, don't do something sensible like read a listings magazine or phone up before hand to find out what time the films start.

❏ If you run into friends whilst on your date, engage them in conversation and don't bother hinting that you'd like them to go, especially if they're doing things that make your date feel uncomfortable, like giggling, whispering, nudging each other and showing no sign of planning to leave.

❏ If any of your date's friends show up, you should sulk until they go away. Be sure to look as po-faced as possible and refuse to respond to any of their efforts to talk to you.

Going for something to eat ...

❑ Take ages to decide what to have.

❑ If your date orders a lot of food, order something very small so that they feel really piggish and uncomfortable while they're eating.

❑ Eat loudly and disgustingly.

❑ Have a long, embarrassing conversation about who's going to pay for what.

Finishing the date ...

❑ If the evening has been an unmitigated disaster, offer to walk your date home anyway. Neither of you will feel able to refuse and you'll have plenty of scope for long, drawn-out silences on the way home, thus allowing for a really horrible end to the evening.

❑ Saying proper goodbyes before you reach the front door means missing out on the enchanting possibility of someone opening the front door and really embarrassing you both. For a nightmare date, all farewells should be left until you arrive at one of your houses, and should involve long, drawn-out spells of hovering in silence.

THIRTEENSOMETHING

❑ If you still like each other, this is where one of you should make confusing, fidgety darting movements in your partner's direction that may or may not be attempts at instigating a kiss. These should be as unclear and confusing as possible.

❑ Continue hovering/making confusing, fidgety darting movements until someone opens the door.

❑ Mumble something that sounds vaguely like goodnight, possibly adding a stupid and embarrassing aside that you can kick yourself over for weeks.

Chapter Three

FOOD

THE AVERAGE DIET OF A TEENAGER

Last year, some nutritional boffins set out to discover exactly what the average teenager in the United Kingdom ate on a day - to - day basis. What they discovered was pretty darn scary stuff. Girls came out slightly worse in the nutrition stakes than boys.
 The average daily menu looked something like this:

BREAKFAST
Nothing

LUNCH
A fizzy drink, a burger, chips

SNACK
Chocolate or crisps

DINNER
A few mouthfuls of whatever is served up at home

Not exactly bursting with goodness, eh? But lots of people seem to be surviving like this, so what's wrong with it?

Well, funny you should ask, but the same boffins also came across a teenage girl with these typical eating habits, who turned out to be suffering from a condition known as scurvy. Scurvy is best known for being

something that sailors and other seafarers suffered from in previous centuries, because they lived on a diet that consisted largely of salty biscuits. It was wiped out when someone had the bright idea of taking boxes of fruit to sea to provide everyone with much needed vitamins and minerals. The fact that scurvy looks set to make a comeback in today's teenagers is not an especially jolly thought to dwell on really, is it?

So What Is A Healthy Diet?

Eating well doesn't necessarily have to mean giving up fast food, snacks and sweets. These are foods which provide little nourishment for your body, so they're not much use, but as long as the rest of your diet is healthy, there's no reason why you shouldn't have a bit of junk food when you fancy it, now and again.

Nutritionists agree that a healthy diet is a well - balanced diet. This basically means eating foods from every food group (i.e. proteins, fats, carbohydrates) every day, in just the right proportions. Very few people follow the exact nutritional guidelines for a balanced diet - in fact, most people probably aren't sure exactly what they are ! - but the closer you can get to striking the right balance, the healthier you'll be, guaranteed !

FOR A BALANCED DIET, TRY TO EAT THE FOLLOWING EVERY DAY...

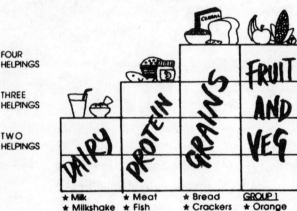

FOUR HELPINGS

THREE HELPINGS

TWO HELPINGS

DAIRY — PROTEIN — GRAINS — FRUIT AND VEG

To get all the vitamins you need from fruit and vegetables, try to choose one helping from each group (see below)

DAIRY
★ Milk
★ Milkshake
★ Cottage-cheese
★ Yogurt
★ Ice-cream
★ Cheese

PROTEIN
★ Meat
★ Fish
★ Poultry
★ Shellfish (e.g. prawns)
★ Liver
★ Eggs
★ Beans
★ Peas
★ Nuts
★ Lentils
★ Peanut butter

GRAINS
★ Bread
★ Crackers
★ Cereal
★ Porridge
★ Pasta
★ Pancakes

GROUP 1
★ Orange
★ Grapefruit
★ Melon
★ Strawberry
★ Tomato
★ Broccoli
★ Peppers
★ Potato
★ Cauliflower

GROUP 2
★ Spinach
★ Carrots
★ Apricots
★ Peaches

GROUP 3
★ Lettuce
★ Courgette
★ Cucumber
★ Corn
★ Beetroot
★ Green-beans
★ Apples
★ Pears
★ Peaches
★ Cherries
★ Berries
★ Bananas

Going Veggie

In this country alone there are over three million vegetarians and nearly half of them are under 16 years old. Every year, thousands of people take the plunge into veggiedom for all sorts of reasons.

Most often it's because they don't approve of killing animals, or because they want to follow a healthier diet, and sometimes it's because they just don't like the taste of meat, or because they have strong political feelings about grain being grown to feed the animals we eat when there are starving humans who need it more. In theory, what you choose to eat (or not eat) should be entirely up to you, but in reality, people often find that the path to meat-free living can be a tricky one to negotiate. Being properly prepared makes things much easier, so if you're planning to say bye - bye to meat, here's everything you need to do to make it as simple as possible.

Four steps towards becoming vegetarian

Decide what kind of veggie you want to be

The usual meaning of the word "vegetarian" is someone who doesn't eat any meat, poultry, game, fish or seafood

- basically anything that was once alive. Simple so far, eh? Many vegetarians also avoid anything containing ingredients made from the above, such as stocks and animal fat. Some also cut out eggs, and stricter vegetarians keep a sharp eye out for things made with less obvious animal ingredients, like puddings containing gelatine, and cheeses made with rennet, a substance that comes from cows' stomachs (unless a cheese is clearly marked as vegetarian, you can assume that it contains rennet). A vegan is the strictest kind of veggie. Apart from all of the above, they also avoid dairy products like milk and butter.

Actually there are stricter people than vegans, but then you're straying into slightly barmy territory with folks who call themselves Fruitarians and eat mainly nuts, grains and fruit, refusing to eat any vegetable that has to be pulled up from the ground (like carrots and potatoes) because they believe that it's cruel to the plants! On the other end of the scale, there are many, many vegetarians who eat fish and seafood, and other people who give up eating red meat (usually for health reasons) but carry on eating poultry and fish. The point is that you shouldn't feel that it's an "all or nothing" situation where you have to change your eating habits all in one go - it's perfectly OK to try things out and decide what suits you best.

Sort out the details of your diet

It's all very well comforting yourself with the thought
that you can still eat pizza and chips and ice-cream
when you become vegetarian, but if that's all you eat,
you'll be on the rocky road to bad health in no time.
Vegetarians *are* generally healthier than meat-eaters, but
it's not just because they're avoiding all the fat and
chemicals in meat - they generally eat more nutritious
food, too. When you give up meat, it's essential to eat
lots of vegetables and fruit, as well as stuff like rice,
porridge, cereal, lentils, beans, nuts and, if you're not
giving up dairy products, cheese and eggs.

Obviously you're going to have to liaise with whoever
is in charge of cooking in your house about your change
of diet, which could be tricky. People who aren't
familiar with vegetarian food often believe the myths
that it's boring, expensive and only available at health-
food shops. In fact most large supermarkets stock
delicious things like veggie burgers, Quorn, and soya-
protein "sausages", cans of chick-peas, dried lentils and
even ready-prepared frozen meals.

Even if you don't have access to a big shop, staples like
baked potatoes, rice, baked beans, nuts and, of course,
vegetables are easy to come by. In most cases these
things actually work out cheaper than meat, and one
look at a vegetarian cook book will prove to any
doubting chef that veggie food is far from dull or

limited. If your parents are concerned that they'll have to cook one meal for you and one for everyone else, you can suggest that your family might enjoy trying some veggie food, offer to cook for yourself (heating up a veggie burger isn't exactly difficult) or point out that lots of dishes (like casseroles, stroganoff, chilli, spaghetti and lasagne) can easily be made in two batches, one without meat.

Prepare to deal with other people

For some reason people can be incredibly unsupportive when you tell them you're deciding to turn vegetarian. Prepare for unhelpful comments, like "What's the point of giving up meat if you'll still eat fish? Fish are living creatures too!" or "But you wear leather shoes!"

Some helpful pointers for you ...

★ Fish don't suffer anywhere near as much as animals that are slaughtered for meat.

★ Fish don't eat grain that could feed humans.

★ If you're being taunted by a non-vegetarian, tell them where to get off right away: whatever you're doing, it's more than they are!

★ If it's a vegetarian giving you hassle, point out that they will never live in an ideal world where everyone is vegetarian if they are so discouraging to people who are willing to convert - they should simply be glad that you're on the right path.

★ If you really want to shut the critics up swiftly, get a pair of plastic or fabric shoes!

Inform your school

If you don't eat packed lunches and your school cafeteria offers few or no vegetarian options, you're perfectly within your rights to take the subject up with your head teacher. If you get a point - blank refusal, you could write off to the Vegetarian Society asking for information about *Choice*, the right to choose vegetarian meals at school campaign. They can supply you with petition forms, which may be the only way you'll get a result. Their address is:

> The Vegetarian Society,
> Parkdale, Dunham Road,
> Altrincham, Cheshire
> WA14 4QG

EATING DISORDERS - WHAT'S THE DEAL?

Bad diets and vegetarianism aren't the only food issues that affect our generation - these days we hear so much about eating disorders that most of us know at least a little bit about them. We've all heard of anorexia and bulimia, but having an eating disorder can also mean over-eating, bingeing or compulsive dieting. The scary official figures show that roughly eight out of ten girls and just over three in ten boys have suffered from some form of eating disorder, which, in real terms, means the chances are high that you either know a sufferer, or are one yourself. Even so, you may still not be clear on just what all the technical jargon means, so here are the bare facts in brief:

Anorexia

What it is: People who suffer from this condition are obsessive about losing weight. They slim by virtually starving themselves, but even when they become painfully thin, they feel that they are still not thin enough. Anorexics hate eating, especially in front of other people, and hate their bodies. They are generally incredibly unhappy.

Why it happens: Anorexics are often people who feel pressure on them to succeed (perhaps because of having ambitious parents or a particularly "perfect" sibling), people who are perfectionists, people who dislike themselves intensely or people (especially girls) faced with puberty who are afraid of "growing up".

The dangers: Anorexia is possibly the most dangerous disorder. You get ill from malnutrition, weak from losing too much weight, can seriously damage your liver and kidneys and permanently weaken your bones. Anorexics usually have to be hospitalised when their weight reaches a dangerously low level and, sadly, a frighteningly high proportion of sufferers die, usually of heart failure, if they are not cured of their condition.

Bulimia

What it is: People with bulimia make themselves throw up after they've eaten, and/or take huge doses of laxatives so that their food goes straight through their body - the medical word for this is "purging". Bulimics often "binge" as well - this means they stuff themselves with really large amounts of food all in one go, usually in secret. Some sufferers also exercise compulsively to "work off" what they eat. Bulimics usually manage to stay at a fairly normal body weight. Because of this, and because they do all their bingeing and purging in secret, their families and friends often don't realise that there is a problem.

Why it happens: Bulimics are often people who feel that they have no control in their lives, and can only stop their feelings of helplessness a little bit by "controlling" their weight.

The dangers: Bulimia can cause all sorts of medical problems, including terrible damage to the stomach, muscle cramps and spasms, swollen glands and rotted teeth (due to the acid produced in vomit). Serious or prolonged cases can result in liver failure and even death.

Compulsive eating

What it is: Compulsive eaters are basically people who over-eat. Like bulimics they often binge, but they don't purge afterwards, so they tend to be overweight. This makes them very unhappy, but they tend to eat even more when they're feeling down, so the problem gets worse and worse. Compulsive eating is not the same as having a big appetite or just liking to eat lots of food - in fact compulsive eaters rarely enjoy eating because it makes them feel guilty and disgusted with themselves.

Why it happens: Compulsive eating is usually a side-effect of an emotional problem of some sort - anything from personal problems like depression, loneliness or insecurity to family problems like an alcoholic parent or child-abuse.

The dangers: Physically, being over-weight is only a health hazard when it's really extreme. Unless they are truly obese, the worst dangers that compulsive eaters face are emotional ones, like getting chronic depression.

Compulsive dieting

What it is: Basically, compulsive dieting means that you go on a diet, lose weight, put it back on, then go on another diet, over and over again. Compulsive dieters don't usually put the weight back on deliberately, it's something that's unavoidable because the only way to lose weight and keep it off is to lose weight gradually by changing your eating habits permanently. Although compulsive dieters think a lot about their appearance, they also get obsessed with dieting itself, and while on the one hand, they diet to "punish" themselves for gaining weight, they also get addicted to the sense of control and achievement that dieting gives them. The fact that they perpetually "fail" at dieting (i.e. they put the weight back on) makes them feel very bad about themselves, which keeps the whole cycle going.

Why it happens: Compulsive dieters are usually not horribly overweight to start with, but feel inadequate anyhow. They mostly have a funny relationship with food, too: they love eating it, and think about it all the time, but hate themselves when they do.

The dangers: Compulsive dieters usually favour crash diets (where you lose fairly large amounts of weight quickly). These are extremely dangerous to your health. Most diets are usually not well balanced, either, so there's a danger of malnutrition, too, and losing and gaining weight over and over again puts a strain on your body.

Can eating disorders be cured?

The answer is yes, but only if you admit that you have a problem and want to be cured. Eating disorders are hardly ever actually about vanity - they're caused by emotional problems, and because of this, can only really be cured by tackling whatever problems caused them in the first place. Serious cases will almost certainly need the professional help of a psychologist or counsellor (your GP should be able to refer you to one). Even if you feel that your situation is not serious, talking your problems through with the school psychiatrist or even a sympathetic relative is the answer.

Sometimes eating disorders (especially compulsive dieting) really are about weight and hating the way your body looks. People in this situation need to learn to like themselves the way they are. If you can do this, you'll find you can let yourself eat the things you like without guilt, and stop eating for reasons other than hunger. The amazing result is usually that any genuine excess weight goes away by itself.

EATING DISORDERS ... AS ADVERTISED ON TV!

Even if you don't *think* that TV, films, magazines and newspapers influence the things you do, the chances are that you could be wrong. Researchers at the University of Birmingham proved in scientific tests that seeing images of very slim, attractive people made people judge themselves far more harshly and less accurately. They also pointed out that bulimia and compulsive dieting had never been heard of until 30 years ago, when it suddenly became fashionable for models and actresses to be very thin. Anorexia increased dramatically at the same time, and the situation has been getting worse ever since. The messages we get from the media are quite confusing: on the one hand, they tell us all about the horrors of bulimia and anorexia, on the other, they show us photos of people

like Princess Diana (who reportedly suffered from both) and comment on what a great, trim figure she has. It's not just girls who are badly affected by these mixed messages: there is a serious, growing problem of teenage boys abusing steroids - highly dangerous drugs that visibly increase the body's muscle mass - because they want to bulk up their physiques.

The media reports the dangers, yet they present ultra-muscled men like Arnold Schwartzenegger, Jean Claude Van Damme and wrestling stars as heroes. Regardless of whether these men use steroids (all of them claim not to, by the way), it's the desire to be like them and the fear of being "puny" that has driven thousands of boys to risk their health using these drugs. Mixed messages in the media are dangerous because by making us feel that we should be thin or brawny, then telling us all about eating disorders and steroid abuse, it's almost like giving us detailed instructions for a quick solution. Often, stable teenagers assume that because they don't have emotional problems, they can safely use the "tricks" they've seen. The fact is that regardless of *why* you do it, messing with your body is intensely dangerous, and never, ever worth the risk.

Chapter Four

Ps And Qs

Dear Ms. Manners,

   Surely in this day and age, manners aren't something I have to think about? I mean, isn't etiquette all about what to say if you have to tell the Queen that the Queen Mother is on the phone or something? Surely this has nothing to do with me? What the hell is this chapter doing here?

Scornful, Dorset

Dear Scornful,

   It's true: etiquette, in the traditional sense of the word, certainly is a load of old guff out of the dark ages that has nothing to do with any of us. When I say manners, I'm not talking about all the stuff you're thinking of (incidentally, the correct way to tell the Queen that the Queen Mother is on the phone would be "Your Majesty, Her Majesty, Your Majesty" - aren't you glad you know that now? It could come in very handy.) I'm talking about behaving in a certain, basic way that makes people warm to you, makes others feel comfortable and, at the end of the day, gets you results. It's surprising how much manners affect our everyday lives. Just read some of the letters I've received recently from people just like you...

Dear Ms. Manners,

My best friend's parents are taking her to a posh restaurant for her birthday, and I'm invited. I'm a bit afraid that I won't know what to do. Help!

Nervous, Oxford

Dear Nervous,

Chill out! Going to a posh restaurant is no big deal. Just follow these simple rules:

1) Don't sit down at the table right away - first ask your friend's parents where they'd like you to sit.

2) Don't get daunted by all the cutlery - just start from the outside and work inwards, changing implements with every course (stop when you reach the salt and pepper shakers).

3) Lay your napkin on your lap before you start eating and put it back on the table at the end.

4) Don't start eating until everyone else has been served their food.

5) Try to eat at the same pace as everyone else.

6) Avoid common social *faux pas* like stealing things, throwing food, burping, or cleaning your nails with your fork (this should be done with the butter knife - no, just kidding!).

7) Don't forget to say thank you afterwards.

8) Above all, enjoy yourself - it's meant to be a celebration, not a test!

Dear Ms. Manners,

One of my friends has really bad B.O. I feel awful because everybody talks about it behind her back, but we're too embarrassed to say anything to her face. I don't want to upset her. What can I do?

Concerned, Devon

Dear Concerned,

As her friend, you're well within your rights, manners wise, to drop her the hint, and you'll be doing her a huge favour. Resist the temptation to do it with the back-up of your other friends - it might be easier for you, but it'll be ten times worse for her, as she'll not only have to cope with the revelation, but also the fact that you've obviously all been discussing it. The simplest way to broach the subject is to drop hints. Try: "You know, my hormones must be going mad, because if I don't wash and use deodorant every morning, my armpits get really smelly!" If she's sharp, she'll cotton on. If she isn't, you might have to add "Do you find yours do, too?" If this still doesn't work, then you'll have to tell her outright, in the gentlest way possible. Saying "Look, I'm sorry, but here's the deal: you smell" is probably not it. Try: "This is very hard for me to say, and I don't think anyone else has noticed it, but I think once or twice you might have forgotten to put on your deodorant in the morning..." This minimises embarrassment and credits her with the intelligence to use a deodorant (even though she probably doesn't). She may still get stroppy initially, but she should be grateful eventually. If she holds it against you permanently, she doesn't understand friendship, and you could probably be forgiven for telling her that actually she pongs to high heaven and everybody knows it.

71

THIRTEENSOMETHING

Dear Ms. Manners,

I've been seeing a very nice girl, and she's invited me to meet her parents. How can I make a good impression?

Anxious, London

Dear Anxious,

The first hurdle is the introductions. Hopefully your girlfriend will do the honours, but if she doesn't, just say "Hello, I'm Anxious, pleased to meet you." You may want to hold out your hand while you say this (in the "shaking hands" position rather than the "high five" position), or a simple smile and a nod will do fine. Addressing your girlfriend's parents as Mr. and Mrs. Whatever always goes down a treat. If they tell you to call them by their first names, it's polite to do so after that. The rest is easy: say please and thank you, wait to be invited to sit down, listen politely when other people are talking, comment on how lovely the food is (even if it isn't) and say "thank you for having me". Apart from all that, just be your sweet self and avoid doing anything that could make your girlfriend's parents feel uncomfortable, (e.g.) arguing with them, saying "Blimey, this place is a bit posh - you must be loaded!", or snogging or groping their daughter). Good luck!

Dear Ms. Manners,

I read your B.O. letter with interest because my form-teacher has a terrible B.O. problem, and although some thoughtful pupils have written numerous hints on the walls of the boys' loos, he still hasn't done anything about it. Apart from the smell, he's very nice and I don't like to hear my classmates making fun of him.

Sympathetic, Brighton

Dear Sympathetic,

Hold your breath when he's nearby and block your ears when people are talking about him. No matter how worthy your motives are and no matter how you put it, telling your teacher he's a bit whiffy is just not on, manners-wise. Sorry!

Dear Ms. Manners,

I was wondering if the above advice would go for telling my teacher that she has lipstick on her teeth. She always does, and everyone laughs about it. Would it be rude of me to mention that?

Concerned, Liverpool

THIRTEENSOMETHING

Dear Concerned,

Mentioning it briefly when there's no one else around is polite and thoughtful behaviour. Holding up your hand in the middle of a lesson and loudly bellowing "'Scuse me Miss! You've got something funny all over your teeth!," is not.

Dear Ms. Manners,

I've recently become vegetarian, and I'm worried about eating at other people's houses. I don't want to be rude or cause trouble, but I really don't want to eat any meat, even to be polite.Determined Veggie, Birmingham

Dear Determined Veggie,

First, make sure that everyone knows that you've turned veggie before you visit (after all, they're not psychic). If someone still cooks you meat, you don't have to eat it to be polite, but you do have to be polite not to eat it, if you see what I mean. Simply explain that you've become vegetarian, say how delicious the food looks and smells (even if it actually makes you want to puke), thank them for going to all the trouble of making it, and apologise profusely for being unable to eat it. Finally, say that you'll be perfectly happy to eat just some vegetables, rice, chips or whatever else has been made to go with the meat.Never point at the dish and scream "Eeeeuuggghhh! Dead animal!," and never try to persuade anyone else in the room not to eat it. If the person who cooked the meal says they'll make you a sandwich or something instead, it's polite to turn down the offer, because it's more work for them. If you're utterly starving, though, you could offer to make the sandwich yourself. Finally, don't discuss your vegetarianism over the meal - the sooner the subject is dropped, the more comfortable the situation will be for everyone.

Dear Ms. Manners,

The new boy at my school, is really nice but also quite wild. He stayed at my house a couple of weeks ago, and it got a bit tricky because he wanted to ask some girls round. I said my parents wouldn't like it and that was that, but now he's asked me to his place. I want to go because he's a laugh, but I don't want to hang around with these girls he knows. The problem is that if it's his house, surely I'd be rude not to do what he wants. Should I just not go?

Unsure, Darlington

Dear Unsure,

It *would* be a bit rude to refuse to do what he wants. If you tell him what you do and don't want to do *before* you agree to go, though, then it's him that's being rude if he goes against your wishes once you're there, and you're well within your rights to say something about it.

Dear Ms. Manners,

My Mum's new boyfriend is quite nice most of the time, but he keeps teasing me about my voice breaking. It makes me even more self - conscious than I am already, and I hate it. I want to tell him to stop it, but I don't want him or my mum (who thinks I'm over-reacting) to think I'm rude. Help!

Frustrated, Edinburgh

Dear Frustrated,

Actually it's your mum's boyfriend who's being rude by making you feel uncomfortable. If you can't persuade your mum to help, just pick a quiet moment and explain nicely that you wish he wouldn't tease you so much - this is not rude behaviour at all and hopefully it'll do the trick.

Dear Ms. Manners,

I asked this girl for a date, and then realised I haven't got enough cash to take her anywhere. Is it rude to ask her to pay for herself?

Skint, Dublin

Dear Skint,

"Going Dutch" is just fine, but it's a bit dodgy to *insist* on going Dutch - you should at least be offering to pay for her because it was *you* who asked *her* out (it would work the same the other way round). The best way out would be to explain that you're short of cash, so you can't do anything expensive when you go out. If she offers to pay for herself, great. If she doesn't, then give her the choice of putting the date off until you've got some cash, or else doing something that doesn't cost anything (like going to the park or coming round to your place to watch a video or play computer games). This way you're being polite and up - front with her, and unless she's a bit of a cow, she should appreciate that and not let it change her opinion of you.

THIRTEENSOMETHING

Dear Ms. Manners

I've been on seven dates with this boy, but he's never tried to kiss me once. My friends think I should make the first move, but I can't help thinking that if he wanted to kiss me, he'd have done it by now. What should I do?

Amorous, Milton Keynes

Dear Amorous,

If you're asking "Is it okay for a girl to kiss a boy first?" then the answer is yes, of course. If you're asking "Is it okay for someone to kiss someone who might not want to be kissed?" then the answer is not really - no one should feel forced into kissing. However, I suspect this boy likes you (or he wouldn't have gone on so many dates with you) and is just shy, in which case he'll probably be thrilled if you kiss him. Try putting your arm round him first - if he seems happy, then he'll probably be keen to have a kiss, too.

Dear Ms. Manners,

My Granny has given me a horrible sweater for my birthday which I'm never going to wear. Now every time I see her, she asks why I'm not wearing it. What can I say?

Miserable owner of a horrible sweater, Glasgow

Dear Miserable owner of a horrible sweater,

The easiest solution is to tell her that it didn't fit, and you want to change it for one in your size, so you'll need the receipt. Then take it back to the shop, change it for something you like and tell her that they didn't have any sweaters left in your size, so you had to change it for something else. If she knitted it herself, however, just wear it next time you see her (you can swiftly remove it as soon as you're out of her sight). Once she's seen you in it and you've told her how much you love it (just a small white lie!), you've politely fulfilled your duty, and you don't have to worry about it again.

79

Chapter Five

MONEY ... OR LACK OF IT

The exceptionally observant among you might notice
when you finish this chapter that it's the shortest in the
book. This might be a coincidence, or it might have
something to do with the fact that although money
comes pretty high up on every adolescent's list of
priorities, there's never as much of it around as you'd
like, and there are hardly any ways around this dismal
fact. Until you leave full-time education, the bulk of
your dosh is going to come from your parents, and these
days, what with the recession, they've probably not got
a lot to chuck around. This is a huge pain, and sadly,
pretty much the end of the story - hence the length of
this chapter.

  It's interesting to note, though, that if you bother to
analyse your feelings towards cash, it's probably not
actually the money itself that you're after - I mean, you
don't want to start a huge savings account or buy a

house or anything like that. What you're really yearning for is the freedom that money gives you to do and buy the things you want. If you don't want to work, there's no miraculous way to spirit cash out of thin air (if I knew of one I'd have written a book on that instead and no doubt be sunning myself on some remote island right now on the proceeds). What I can divulge, however, are a few tips on how to make the little money you have access, to stretch a little further. Yes indeed, with a dash of planning and cunning, you can greatly improve your chances of getting your mitts on most of the things you want...

TEENAGE LIFE ON ROUGHLY NOUGHT P A DAY ... HOW TO GET STUFF WITHOUT BREAKING THE (PIGGY) BANK

1) Getting maximum mileage out of birthdays and Christmas

Occasions when people give you presents are your best opportunity for getting what you want, because these are the times of year when the people who love you really want to buy you something you'll like. This may seem painfully obvious, but ask yourself if you *really* make the most of it? Do you get a few things you like, a few things you don't, and then spend the rest of the year wishing for other stuff?

THIRTEENSOMETHING

When you were little, getting surprises was half the
fun, but these days it's well worth considering giving up
this thrill and asking nicely for specific things you want
instead. It's often tempting to ask for money - after all,
it means you don't have to work out what you want
right away - but this does take some of the fun out of
the occasion for your relatives. A better bet for everyone
would be for you to sit down and make a list of things
you'd really love, so that you'll be able to give your
relatives some ideas for presents. You could even have a
"wants" list running all year, so that you don't have to
make rash decisions come celebration time. When
you're thinking about things you want, don't limit
yourself to concrete things - remember great treats like
a subscription to your favourite magazine, and tokens
for all sorts of things from music, books and clothes to
the cinema and even fast food places. They're good news
for your relatives because they're more like a proper
present than plain old money, and good news for you
because they give you some of the freedom of choice
that cash can.

If you're hankering for something really huge and
expensive, you could mention it to your parents, adding
that you know it's too expensive for them to buy, but
suggesting that they could club together with all the
other relatives who wanted to buy you a present in order
to afford it.

2) Get into swapping

When you fancy having new things, you don't necessarily mean things that are *brand new* - just stuff that's new to *you*. With this in mind, starting a big swapping network with your friends and relatives is a most excellent option. Getting your hands on someone else's clothes, books, computer games or videos can be every bit as exciting as getting your hands on brand new stuff, and the great thing is that all the old stuff you're bored stiff with is probably just as thrilling to them. At first swapping can seem a little scary - after all, as much as you want new things, it can be hard to part with your own gear. Don't forget, then, that swapping doesn't have to be permanent - in fact you'll make more swaps if you agree that it's only for a set period of time (a couple of weeks, for instance). If at the end of that time both you and the person you've made the swap, with, both love your new acquisitions and aren't missing the thing you gave away, you can always re-negotiate and either extend the swap time or make it permanent.

3) Get into sharing

I'm not talking about the kind of sharing that your mum used to nag you about when you were little - after

all, if something is yours, you want to have the main use
of it yourself, especially if you saved up for it and
bought it yourself. To work properly, sharing has to be
totally equal and fair. For example, let's say you and two
of your friends all have a burning desire to buy
something - a piece of clothing, a computer game, an
album, whatever - but none of you have enough dough.
The chances are that if you pooled your money, you
could afford to buy it, and then share it. To avoid
argument, you'd have to work out the terms first, like
how many days you'll each have it for, and who'll have it
first (by tossing a coin or drawing straws, for instance).
You've also got to be very thoughtful and sensible when
it comes to your turn to pass it on. If you reckon you
can manage to do those things, then sharing can be a
brilliant way to get things you want on the cheap.

4) Collaborate with your parents

If there's something that you desperately want but you
can't wait for Christmas or your birthday, or no one
wants to buy it for you, it's always worth sitting down
for a serious talk with your parents. You should calmly
tell them how much you'd like it, and explain that
you're prepared to put in 100% effort in saving up
enough money to buy it. Let them know just how
serious you are. If you show enough willing (for

instance, by asking them to hold on to half of each month's pocket money and save it for you) they should feel that your dedication is so commendable that they'll do everything they can to help you save, and might even offer to match your savings with their own money each month.

You could also ask them if there are any ways they can think of that you could earn some more money towards your savings: perhaps they could find you some extra chores that they'd be prepared to pay you for. I know this all sound horribly business-like, but the more determination and maturity you show, the greater the dividends, believe me!

5) Get a job!

Obviously having your own money makes a huge difference in life, and there's nothing quite like the feeling you get when you're holding the first money you've actually earned. However, it's really important to do plenty of serious thinking and planning before you get involved in any kind of work. Here are the plain facts:

★ If you're under 13, you can't legally work in a part-time job, so if you're still determined to earn money, your only options are casual jobs for neighbours and your parents' friends, like washing cars or baby-sitting. If you get a baby - sitting job, always take important precautions like having the phone numbers of a doctor and the place where the child's parents are going to be.

★ If you're over 13 you can work legally part-time in shops or doing delivery rounds, as long as you don't start work before 7 a.m. or finish after 7 p.m. You're not allowed to work for more than two hours on any Sunday or school day and in some areas, you can't work for more than four hours on a Saturday or in school holidays.

★ The law says that under-18s can't work on ships, in factories, in mines or quarries, on construction sites or on any job that takes place on the street, such as selling newspapers or flowers, busking or working on a market stall (unless you're working for a parent or guardian).

★ Under-16s aren't allowed to do manual work of any kind, including jobs in shops or offices which might involve lifting or moving heavy things. They're also not allowed to work with, move or even *clean* dangerous machinery.

★ When you find the right job, you should check it out with your local authorities, as they might need to give you a special permit or employment card before you start.

★ The minute you start working for someone, it legally means you have entered into a contract with them. This means that you have agreed to the terms of employment they've told you about, so never start work until you're crystal clear about, and perfectly happy with, the details your employer has given you about your pay, your hours of work and any other details like holiday entitlements.

★ If you work more than 16 hours a week for the same employer and you've been working for them for 13 weeks or more, you are legally entitled to ask for (and get!) a written statement of conditions, telling you about your wages, hours and conditions of employment.

★ It's a horrible fact that there are no laws about minimum pay for under-16s, and lots of badly-paid young people are afraid to ask for a rise in case they get the sack. Sadly, many employers do choose to find someone new who is willing to work for the same wage rather than give a rise.

★ If you're given the sack unfairly, or have to work over-long hours, your Education Welfare Officer at the local education authority could help. You could also contact the Children's Legal Centre at 20 Compton Terrace, London N1 2UN or the Low Pay Unit at 9 Upper Berkeley Street, London W1H 8BY.

Chapter Six

YOUR ROOM

YOUR FIRST BRUSH WITH INTERIOR DECORATING

When you were little, your room was just somewhere you happened to sleep. Now it's so much more - after all, it's the only place on the planet right now that's truly *yours*. It's your territory, your space, your own little sanctuary from the often mystifying outside world where every other place you have to spend time in is owned and decorated by somebody else. Because of this, the way your room looks is very important. You are no longer a kid, and you want it to reflect your personality as it is now. This is most likely going to mean saying bye - bye to the quilted wall-hanging depicting Winnie-The-Pooh holding a balloon, and hello to lots of nice shiny posters ripped out of magazines. All well and good so far, but there's so much more that you want to do. You'll scream if you have to spend one more night under that Ghostbusters duvet you begged your parents for when you were eight. You've got thousands of ideas and a budget of roughly nought p. Nightmare, eh? But stay calm and read on. With a little planning, the room of your dreams could become a reality.

The Totally Foolproof Guide To Decorating

Before you start ...

★ You may think that you know exactly how you want your room to be, but before you do anything, stop for a minute and make a proper plan. You're probably clearer on what you *don't* want (i.e. everything that's there at the moment) than what you do want, and although this can be fairly handy, it won't actually get you anywhere. The urge to get started immediately may seem enormous, but you're guaranteed more satisfaction in the long run if you take the time to really plan ahead. This is firstly because you'll end up with what you really want, and secondly because you'll be more likely to achieve a total overhaul of your room if you approach your parents or piggy bank with a proper breakdown of a budget for *everything* you want, rather than madly campaigning for one thing after another only to discover halfway through that there's no more cash to be had. If you share your room with a brother or sister, then there's nothing for it but to get them involved at this stage too, unless they're totally disinterested and prepared to give you a free hand.

★ Start your plan by jotting down anything that comes into your head. Then, if you're short on inspiration, take the time to look around. Furniture catalogues and interior decorating magazines are great for getting ideas. (Even if the actual things featured are beyond your pocket, the chances are you could get the same effect on the cheap.) Check out local shops for curtains and wallpaper.

★ You don't even have to go out of your way to get inspiration - if you just keep decorating in the back of your mind at all times, you're bound to pick something up. Take an extra close look at other people's rooms when you go visiting, when you watch TV or movies or when you read magazines, and you never know what you might spot. Keep a notebook with you to write ideas in, and in no time, you'll be ready to piece together your first proper plan.

★Your first draft of the plan needn't take cost into consideration - make it your ultimate wants list. Working out how to cut corners comes later. Now work out roughly how much it'll all cost, and when you've arrived at a figure, it's time for a chat with your parents.

★ The first chat with your parents is the most important. Your approach counts for everything. Just imagine you were an adult going to see a bank manager about a loan. Would you turn up looking surly? Would you have the attitude that it wouldn't be a favour but your *right* to get the money from him? Would you accuse him of being stingy? Obviously not. You'd know automatically that the more polite, respectful and sensible you were, the more likely you'd be to leave triumphant.Considering that your parents have spent money on you for your entire life and never once demanded repayment with interest, it would make sense that you treat them with at least the same measure of courtesy that you'd treat a bank manager, if not more. The main rules to remember if you want things to go your way are: no whining, no demands, no emotional blackmail, no accusations of unfairness; but buckets of gratitude, huge displays of reasonable behaviour and lots of willingness to compromise.Make it clear that you're prepared to put in the work if necessary (painting, making things, shopping) and do anything else they feel needs doing (like cleaning up or sorting out your old stuff first). Promising to chip in your own savings or future pocket money is also a winner because it shows that you're prepared to make sacrifices, and is the best and most pleasant way to demonstrate just how much this redecorating lark means to you (as opposed to an Oscar-worthy display of crying, screaming and stamping which also makes it pretty clear, but won't win you any brownie points).

If all goes well, you'll come away with a rough budget figure to work around.

★ If your parents tell you that they can't possibly afford *anything* right now, they're probably telling the truth and if you want to be in with a shout when the family finances finally perk up, it's a good idea to accept this graciously rather than sulk and mutter darkly that your nice, loving parents have obviously been abducted by aliens and replaced by loathsome, miserly monsters from the planet Vile who want to torment you.

★ When you've got some figures to juggle with, it's time to go back to your list and work out what goes, what stays and what changes - sure, you wish you could have it all (it *was* a wish list, remember?) but that's life. Forget it. Just do it. If you do it well, there's no reason why any of your ideas has to end up in the bin - there's usually a cheap way round things if you look hard enough.

Some cheap ideas for starters ...

★ Brand new curtains are expensive, but it's not that hard to make your own. If you're utterly useless at sewing, you can get great effects by just draping lengths of material over the existing rail.

★ Check out craft shops, haberdashers and even Indian sari centres for interesting and cheap dress-making fabrics to make your curtains with.

★ If you can't find bed-linen you like, why not buy something cheap in a pale colour and dye it - or give your own linen a new lease of life the same way. Craft shops and haberdashers have easy-to-use fabric dyes in loads of colours, and dye-pens that are great for drawing on designs.

★ For a hippyish look, you could tie-dye your bed-linen (grab a handful of fabric, secure tightly with rubber bands or string and repeat all over before dyeing the whole lot, or even dipping the secured bobbles of fabric into different bowls of dye for a multi-coloured effect).

★ New carpet is dead expensive, so the chances are that you won't be getting any. If your existing flooring is *really* vile though, you may feel that it's worth sacrificing a few of the other things you were planning to get in order to afford it. Some carpet shops offer cheap deals on leftovers.

★ Look for rugs - you might find a nice one that's big enough to hide most of the visible floor once the furniture's been moved round a bit.

★ Check out car-boot sales, second-hand shops and advertisements in the local paper for furniture.

★ Doll-up second hand furniture or revamp your existing stuff by getting creative with paint. Some household brands come in smaller-sized pots, which is handy for keeping costs down.

★ You don't have to go for the obvious and match furniture, floor and wall colours - I once saw a room painted bright white with every piece of furniture painted a different outrageously bright colour and it looked amazing.

★ Exterior metal paints like Hammerite give a stunning unusual metallic effect.

★ A good trick to try is buying three small pots of paint in different shades, painting the lightest shade all over, then using a natural sea sponge to apply the other two on top. Use three shades of the same colour for a subtle, marbled effect or go for something dramatic like white, grey and black or yellow, orange and dark brown.

★ The boring bit: no matter how careful you intend to be, always put newspaper down to protect the floor - or better still, move the furniture outside or into a garage and do it there.

★ Don't fancy painting? Draping lengths of nice material over furniture can look brilliant too.

★ Posters are cheap, effective and a great way to surround yourself with images that make you happy and that say something about who you are and what you like. If you want a neater, sleeker look for your new room, you could always buy a large cork board and confine posters to that (it also means you can chop and change without damaging nice, newly painted walls).

★ A horrible lampshade can make a lot of difference to an otherwise nice room. Luckily, lampshades are cheap to buy (you don't have to replace the whole fitting), and you can customise plain ones with left-over paint.

Getting started

Once you've finalised your plans, bought what you need and cleared up your room in preparation, you're all set. The final things to remember are:

★ There's no way you can get it all done in a day, so don't try. Why not wait until the holidays?

★ Try to stick to your original plan and budget.

★ Decorating a room is a lot of work for one person. If your family aren't involved, why not ask a friend to help? It'll be easier and more fun,

 Good luck!

SHARE AND SHARE ALIKE?

Sharing a bedroom is like getting spots: it's a fact of life that some people just have to deal with and others don't, it doesn't seem too horrendous until it happens to you, and the only comfort is knowing that it'll hopefully all be over by the time you're out of your teens. Unlike having spots, however, there is no cure for having to share a room, except perhaps murder, which is a bit extreme (although there are bound to be times when it seems like quite a viable option). Of course, every situation has benefits as well as drawbacks. There will no doubt be wonderful times when you go to sleep with a big smile on your face after a lovely long giggly, whispery chat with your beloved sibling that's lasted into the wee small hours. Conversely, there will also be times when you go to sleep with a big *scratch* on your face after a not very lovely long fight over who busted the cassette deck. On the whole, people who have to share rooms would rather they didn't, but it's nice to know that like so many less-than-pleasant things (i.e. grilled liver, dentists, school), sharing a room is actually good for you. As any boring old codger you'd care to ask will tell you, it teaches you the meaning of precious virtues like sharing, tolerance and respecting other people's property. Mind you, no one ever said you had to actually practise what you learnt, and you probably won't bother (unless borrowing your brother's new leather jacket without asking and proudly showing it off to all your friends at the school disco counts as respecting other people's property). As with everything in life, you've got to make the best of what you've got. I hope my three golden rules for surviving a room-sharing relationship may help.

RULE 1.

Dividing up a room so that each person has his or her own space is generally a really top idea. On the negative side, however, it can bring out the worst of your animal-like territorial instincts from deep within your psyche, so try to keep things within reason.

RULE 2.

Remember that sharing a room is nothing to be ashamed of. Don't bother trying to impress people by pretending that you don't, because you'll always get found out.

RULE 3.

Try to make the most of the situation by bearing in mind that it brings you companionship and added closeness to your sibling. Failing this, bear in mind that it gives you the opportunity to gather loads of terrific, really embarrassing ammunition to use in years to come.

GET TIDY!

It's incredible to think that just three little words can unleash oceans of emotion, change your entire mood and sum up so many poignant and important things in your mind about your relationship with your parents. No, I'm not talking about *I love you*, I'm talking about *tidy your room*. I have no doubt that parents have been uttering this immortal phrase since the first stone-age teenager got his or her own corner of the cave, and it's been so over-used since that it would be a laughable cliché if it weren't for the fact that generation after generation of parents actually keep on saying it, usually at the top of their voices.

So what's the deal? In the blue corner there are your parents with a major bee in their bonnets about your room being in a mess. In the red corner there's you, puzzled as to why it should concern them when it's not them who has to spend time in it, and utterly convinced that life is far too short to spend much (if any) of it tidying up. The fight ensues, no one wins and a rematch is arranged to take place in the same venue every day for the next decade.

Now, I'm on your side here - I agree entirely that life's too short for tidying up. However, I also think that life's too short for constantly having the same tedious argument over and over again. At the end of the day, your parents are never going to back down because they are parents and parents are bolshy like that and they just can't help it. The simplest thing to do, therefore, would be to tidy your room. Just think about it ... No more nagging. No more arguments. No more parental invasion of privacy on the premise of trying to find a long-lost coffee mug. No more having to suffer crap jokes like "Were those your football socks I just saw crawling towards the laundry basket by themselves?". Sounds good, doesn't it? And that's before we've even considered the possibility of rewards for good behaviour. Now, even if I've sold you on the idea of tidying your room, you've no doubt still branded me a spy sent from the enemy camp. I plead innocent on that charge. You don't honestly think I'd want you to waste your precious time and get all sweaty doing manual labour in your bedroom? No way. I'm here to reveal the possibility of reaping all the benefits of a tidy room with little of the effort. The fact is that it's actually possible to tidy your room in two minutes using a top secret, deeply cunning and preposterously lazy method, which I am about to divulge...

The Top Secret, Deeply Cunning And Preposterously Lazy 120 Second Blitz

You will need:

> a large carrier bag
> a bin bag
> a cardboard box

Step 1

Cluttered surfaces are the number one culprit for making a room look messy, so attack them first. Start by sweeping everything off every surface onto the bed for sorting. First put aside anything you use every day (such as your alarm clock, spectacles etc.) and anything decorative (models, pictures in stand-up frames, ornaments), then pick through what's left and dump obvious items of rubbish (old tissues, crisp packets etc.) in the bin bag. Next, fish out any old cups or plates and leave them outside the bedroom door to be transferred to the kitchen later. Now sweep everything else that's left into the carrier bag and put the carrier bag in your wardrobe or in a drawer (you can leave it there until you feel inclined to sort it out, which will probably be when you leave home, but never mind). Now replace all the ornaments and essential things on the nice clear surfaces.

Step 2

Cluttered floors come just a hair's breadth behind
cluttered surfaces in the bad-appearance stakes. Quickly
pick up everything off the floor and chuck it on the bed,
then as before, pick out and deal with the rubbish and
crockery first. Most of what's left is likely to be clothes,
and if they've been on the floor, let's assume they're
probably dirty, so make a quick run to the laundry
basket to get them all off your hands. Swiftly take stock
of the rest of the floor stuff. Throw any shoes into your
cupboard, put magazines in a neat pile by the side of
your bed (underneath a bedside table is ideal) and put
books onto a shelf along with anything else that belongs
on one. Shove whatever is left on the bed into your
secret carrier bag. If it doesn't fit, hide it under your
bed.

Step 3

If you've got a desk, stack anything on it that's flat
(magazines, textbooks etc.) into a neat pile and tuck the
pile underneath the desk. Put pens in a cup or pen-
holder. Computer debris (like software and add-ons) or
bits from any other hobby can be a nightmare, but
they're easily dealt with by popping the whole lot in
your empty cardboard box and slipping that under the
desk too.

Step 4

Finally, look around. Is there anything still lying about?
If so, shove it under the bed or in the secret carrier bag.
Now make sure all cupboard doors and drawers are shut,
straighten your bedclothes, throw the bin bag into the
hall and hey presto - stand back and enjoy the praise.

The beauty of this method is that it's not only easy to
maintain, but if you ever feel the urge to actually sort
things out more thoroughly, you can do it in easy bite-
sized chunks - the carrier bag one day, the box on
another, the under-bed stash on another and so on.
Enjoy the benefits of your new-found virtue ... but never
reveal your secret formula to the enemy!

CHAPTER SEVEN

YOUR FAMILY

PARENTS - AT LAST, THE TRUTH

Parents and their offspring have generally failed to see eye-to-eye since time immemorial. Decade after decade, perfectly reasonable teenagers grow up baffled by their parents' behaviour and then they have kids of their own and *bingo* - they inexplicably start doing all the same things that *their* parents did to drive *them* mad. Now, I'm well aware that this is a mystery that lots of people have tried to explain before. There have been so many books and magazine articles that try to tell you that your parents are actually really reasonable humans whom you should try to understand and identify with in order to reason with them and understand their annoying habits, embarrassing ways and preposterous behaviour. If you're as sick of hearing all that as I am, you'll be relieved to hear that I have a different set of answers. I have, in fact, unravelled the truth that has been hidden for thousands of years, the simple explanation behind the behaviour of parents everywhere, and now it can be told ...

I have unearthed the top-secret, high-security document distributed by the government to every adult when they become a parent, the super-strict outline of the rules that must be obeyed, and at last everything becomes clear. This is it...

The Parents' Charter

This document is highly confidential.
Do not let anybody see it.

Dear Sir/Madam,

Congratulations on becoming a parent ! We hope you will enjoy your new baby very much. For the first ten years or so, it will be your job to look after it, be nice to it, and generally do the best you can. After that, you will be closely monitored to see that you are adhering to the rules detailed below for parenting pre-teens and teenagers. Please read through them carefully.

THIRTEENSOMETHING

Rule 1. Speak In Clichés.

Every week, you must fulfil a strict quota of phrases from the list below. You must be sure to use at least seven a week to avoid penalty, but you will be paid a bonus of £1 for each additional use over and above the quota. A bonus of £5 will be paid for particularly creative combinations of two or more of the phrases. Choose freely from this list:

★ Tidy your room ! ★ Well we're not everybody else's parents ... ★ When I was your age ... ★ Act your age! ★ Young man/lady ★ Where do you think you're going? ★ We're not made of money ★ Not now, I'm busy ★ Money doesn't grow on trees, you know! ★ What time do you call this? ★ Because I say so ★ Go to your room! ★ Grow up! ★ I'll treat you like an adult when you start acting like one ★ You've got no one to blame but yourself ★ Don't take that tone of voice with me ... ★ Look at me when I'm talking to you ★ How many times have I told you ... ★ Stop feeling sorry for yourself ★ You ought to be ashamed of yourself ★ You're not the only pebble on the beach!

Rule 2. Be Irritating.

Being irritating is an essential part of your job. You will

find that it comes naturally after a while, but to get you started, here are some effective examples of irritating behaviour:

★ Waiting quietly outside your child's bedroom door until you are certain that they are looking in the mirror and miming to a record with a hairbrush, then bursting in to announce that dinner is ready

★ Asking your child to undertake lots of unpleasant household chores when they are busy studying, then saying "Well I was going to suggest we all go to the cinema to see that film you really wanted to see, but I suppose you're too busy studying, so we'll go without you!"

★ Always arranging holidays or family outings so that they fall on the same day as something all your child's friends are doing so that they will be the only one who can't go

Rule 3. Be Embarrassing At All Times.

Humiliating your child is your most important task of all. Try to do it as often as possible, looking for the potential embarrassment-factor in every situation.

The standard methods, however, are as follows:

★ Suggest a discussion about contraception whenever your child mentions a friend of the opposite sex

★ Leave leaflets about contraception lying around, especially if your child is going to have friends in the house

★ Kiss and cuddle affectionately with your spouse as often as you can when your child is present

★ If you are collecting your child from a party, never wait outside. Instead, be sure to arrive early and enter the party shouting your child's name loudly and introducing yourself to everybody.

★ When your child's friends are present it is very important to ask them if they would like to see some photographs of your child as a baby. Even if they do not, you must show them anyway. Photographs of your child sitting on a potty are especially effective in this situation, as are pictures depicting your child nude in the bath. Home video footage is even better.

★ If you should be so fortunate as to discover that your child has a crush on somebody, be sure to tease them about it as often as possible, ideally when other people are present.

★ Dancing at parties, weddings and other social gatherings is your greatest weapon. Practise hard to perfect this important skill.

BASIC STEPS

1. THE TWIST

2. THE POGO

3. 70S DISCO

★ Always dress as strangely as possible in public or when your child's friends are visiting.

★ When making sandwiches for packed lunches, always remove the crusts and cut the sandwich into quarters. If possible, include an affectionate note using the child's babyhood nickname, stating that you have made the sandwich how they like it.

SIBLING PSYCHOLOGY

Many psychologists reckon that the position you hold in your family helps to shape your personality. By position, they mean how many siblings you've got, what sex they are and whether they're younger or older than you. Find out what your family reveals about you, by first reading this list of family positions to discover which type you are ...

If you're a girl and you've got ....

... an older brother and no sisters:	type 1
... a younger brother and no sisters:	type 2
... an older sister and no brothers:	type 3
... a younger sister and no brothers:	type 4
... older and younger sisters, no brothers:	type 5
... older and younger brothers, no sisters:	type 6

If you're a boy and you've got ...

... an older sister and no brothers:	type 1
... a younger sister and no brothers:	type 2
... an older brother and no sisters:	type 3
... a younger brother and no sisters:	type 4
... older and younger brothers, no sisters:	type 5
... older and younger sisters, no brothers:	type 6

If you're either sex and you've got ...

... an older brother and sister, none younger:	type 7
... a younger brother and sister, none older:	type 8
... older and younger sisters and brothers:	type 9
... no brothers or sisters:	type 10

Note: If you're a twin or triplet, count whichever of you was born first as the oldest and work it out from there. Worked it out? Now read on to find out all about your personality type ...

Type 1

Good points: You're likely to be intelligent, popular, talented, and loads of fun to be with. You've got a tough image, but those who know you well know that you're really gentle and sensitive underneath it.

Bad points: You're moody at times, you like to get your own way, and you often expect other people to do things for you and give you attention as and when you want.

Friendship: Your sparkling personality will draw all sorts of people to you, but you'll be most likely to pick friends who'll let you take the lead. Your perfect pal would be someone with an older sibling, or older and younger siblings.

Romance: You like lots of attention and fuss, and you'll be happiest with someone who is strong and confident, but lets you do as you please. Your perfect mate would be someone with younger brothers or sisters.

Type 2

Good points: You're confident, tough and very individual, and when your mind is set on something, you're nearly always able to make it happen. You're very good at looking after the people you care about, and make it your business to help sort out everybody's problems.

Bad points: You can be so determined to get what you want that you don't mind using other people, even your friends, if you have to. You also hate to admit that you're wrong, tend to hide your true feelings, and can be a bit bossy at times!

Friendship: You like to be the boss in your friendships, but those who let you take charge are rewarded with your huge loyalty and support. Your perfect pal would be someone with an older sibling.

Romance: You're a big flirt, and some shy types might find this a bit scary! You'd be happiest with someone as tough and confident as you, who doesn't mind taking charge sometimes, and won't get too jealous when you flirt with other people! Your perfect match would be someone with older and younger siblings of the opposite sex to them.

Type 3

Good points: You've got a great sense of humour and will do anything for a laugh. This, and your friendly, open nature makes you very popular, and you're also kind, generous and easy-going.

Bad points: You can be quite competitive and envious in your friendships, and you often can't be bothered to go out of your way to do things for your friends, either. You also find it very hard to make up your mind about things sometimes.

Friendship: You like your mates to be supportive and reliable, and you like people you can look up to and admire. Your perfect pal would be someone with a younger sibling of the same sex as them.

Romance: You're not very confident around the opposite sex, so you'll definitely need someone who'll make the first move and call all the shots. Even though you're bound to be good fun to go out with, you're bound to constantly worry that your date doesn't like being with you! Your ideal mate would be someone with a younger brother or sister.

Type 4

Good points: You're clever, strong, self-assured and never afraid to stand up for yourself and the things you believe in.

Bad points: You can be a bit bossy, thoughtless and even mean with your friends, and you sometimes feel so afraid of seeming "drippy" that you don't let the people close to you know how much you care about them.

Friendships: You're very protective of your friends and dead loyal, too. You need someone who'll be just as loyal, but prepared to put up with your sometimes careless treatment of them! Your perfect pal is someone with an older sibling.

Romance: If you're dating someone, you expect them to put you first in their list of priorities, and you'll settle for nothing less than 100% attention. You don't like making the first move - or any of the other moves for that matter, so you need someone who will. Your perfect mate would be someone with an older sibling of the same sex as them.

Type 5

Good points: You're an optimistic, happy-go-lucky type who's well-balanced, cheerful, honest and has a great sense of humour.

Bad points: Your honesty can also turn into tactlessness at times, and your cheeky nature can mean that you're not always well-behaved, which spells frequent trouble at school or at home.

Friendship: You hate being alone, so your friends are very important to you. Although you're great at making your friends laugh, you're not always that sensitive when it comes to having a laugh at their expense, so you need people who are very loyal and won't get too upset by your teasing! Your perfect pal is someone with an older and younger sibling of the same sex as them.

Romance: As bubbly and daring as you are, you can get a bit shy around the opposite sex, who are something of a mystery to you. The thought of asking someone out scares you silly, so you either wait for others to make the first move, or make sure you have plenty of friends with you for moral support! You need someone who is fun, gentle and understanding. Your perfect match would be someone with a younger sibling of the opposite sex to them, or an older sibling of the same sex and a younger sibling of the opposite sex.

Type 6

Good points: You're energetic, adventurous and friendly, with plenty of confidence. You especially enjoy hanging out with people of the opposite sex, and you're always popular with them because you understand them so well.

Bad points: You're sometimes a bit of a bully, although at other times you'll let other people take advantage of you. You don't like arguments, but you seem to get into them more often than most!

Friendship: You need well-balanced friends who'll keep things on an equal footing - being nice and kind to you, but not letting you walk all over them! A perfect pal would be someone else with older and younger siblings of the opposite sex to them, or someone with a younger brother or sister.

Romance: You're mighty popular with the opposite sex, and probably have no trouble finding a date. You're looking for someone attentive and adoring, who'll hang onto your every word. Someone with older and younger brothers and sisters would be ideal.

Type 7

Good points: You're a brainy, individual, vivacious type who enjoys being in the limelight. You're very sure of yourself and you find it easy to make friends and get along with people.

Bad points: Your noisy behaviour can often embarrass your friends, but as far as you're concerned, that's their problem! When you're not the centre of attention, or you don't get your own way, you can get a bit sulky and childish.

Friendship: You just want to be liked, which is why you always go out of your way to keep your friends entertained. Even though you sometimes worry about not fitting in, you're happiest when you're with a big gang of friends. Your perfect pal would be someone with a younger sibling of the same sex as them.

Romance: Dating may not be very high on your list of interests, and you can be a bit shy around the opposite sex. When you do find your ideal mate - someone who is fun and understanding - you're always affectionate and faithful to them. Look for someone with a younger brother or sister.

Type 8

Good points: You're sensible, organised, practical and decisive - a very mature character indeed!

Bad points: You've got a rotten temper and you can suffer from big-headedness and bossiness too.

Friendship: You're likeable and friendly most of the time, but you need friends who'll put up with your grumpy moods too. Your perfect pals would be only children and people with older siblings of the same sex.

Romance: You need someone who will adore you, admire you, appreciate you totally, and let you boss them around a bit, too. When you find someone prepared to do all this, you'll make it worth their while by being super-attentive and thoughtful. You're fussy though, and wouldn't go out with just *anyone* - you're waiting for someone special, and if no one available fits the bill, you'd rather just hang out with your mates. Your perfect match is an only child or someone with an older sibling of the opposite sex to them.

Type 9

Good points: You're happy and easy-going, and although you're bound to be very good at many things, you never get big-headed because you often suffer from feelings of insecurity and self-doubt, too.

Bad points: You can be a little bit selfish sometimes and you expect a great deal of attention and loyalty from the people around you, turning quite cool if you don't get it.

Friendship: You're quiet at times, but you've got a clever sense of humour and enjoy keeping your friends laughing when you're in the mood. A perfect pal for you would be an only child or someone with older brothers and/or sisters.

Romance: You're good at chatting people up, but unless you're pretty sure they're interested in you, you won't bother. The thought of going on a date can often panic you, and if things get serious, you'll get even more spooked and often back off, even if you like the person a lot. You need someone who'll make you feel special. An ideal match would be someone with an older sibling of the same sex, or someone who, like you, has older and younger brothers and sisters.

Type 10

Good points: You're imaginative, unconventional and independent. You make very interesting, fun company, and are always full of great ideas.

Bad points: You're impatient, sulky at times, and prone to getting frustrated when people and situations aren't just how you want them to be.

Friendship: As long as your friends fit in with your needs and give you a bit of space when you want it, you're happy. Your perfect pal would be someone with a younger sibling.

Romance: Although you get along well with the opposite sex as friends, you often find dating a very confusing business and go through phases where you're not terribly interested in it at all. When you are, you like people who are mature (possibly older than you), strong and confident, and you need them to pay you lots of attention but never interfere too much with your life. Your ideal match is another only child, or someone with a younger sibling of the opposite sex to them.

Chapter Eight

GROOMING

MIRROR, MIRROR ON THE WALL ...

No one has ever done any research on what proportion of our teenage years we spend staring into a mirror, which is probably just as well, because we'd all be hugely embarrassed by the results. It's bizarre to think that not so long ago, you were perfectly happy to run around with your face covered in mud and snot, wearing a pudding - bowl haircut and ill-fitting clothes your mum chose. Then suddenly you hit a certain age where you discover that the shiny thing in the bathroom actually shows your reflection when you look into it. Welcome to the start of a long and not always easy relationship with the mirror.

The curious thing about mirrors is that what you see in them isn't what others see when they look at you. This is true on two levels. First, you're seeing a reversed image. Then there's also the little-known fact that the longer you look into a mirror, the more mind-blowingly hideous your reflection becomes. This is because we spend so long focusing on all our little imperfections (which everyone else totally fails to notice on a day-to-day basis) that we eventually can't see the overall picture - just the worst bits, magnified.

WHAT THEY SEE...   WHAT YOU SEE...

WHY DON'T I LOOK LIKE THAT?

There also comes a time in everyone's life when you look at the people in magazines, movies or TV shows, and then you look in a mirror, make a calm, calculated comparison, consider your options for self-improvement... and finally decide that crawling under a rock and hiding for the next 50 years seems like the best solution.

There is a very good reason why you don't look like these ludicrously attractive people: they don't look like that either. Now, I'm not trying to tell you that it's all

WHAT YOU SEE...

WHAT YOU DONT SEE ...

camera trickery and your favourite film-star or super-model is actually a hideous slime-beast from the planet Ugly - obviously there *is* a certain measure of attractiveness there to start with. However, even the most gorgeous celebrities and models actually look relatively normal in real life. Ask anyone who's ever met one, and unless they were so totally bowled over that they were blinded to reality, they're bound to express surprise at discovering some sort of glaring imperfection, be it a dodgy complexion, sticky-out ears, minimal height or big feet.

There really, truly is no such thing as perfection in real life. When you see an image of a perfect-looking person, you're actually looking at the toil of a huge team of highly-skilled people, a work of art laboriously created by professionals. Comparing these images with your holidays snaps is like comparing a beautiful oil painting in a museum to your little brother's masterful crayon rendition entitled "Mummy" that mysteriously resembles a spider being crushed by a large orange. Just like the oilpainting, the nice pictures and images are there to be admired. But don't be fooled into thinking they're any truer a reflection of reality.

I'LL JUST DIE IF I DON'T HAVE THEM!

If you stop and think about it, the invention of expensive "brand-name" clothes was one of the worst things that happened in the '80s. All of a sudden it wasn't just what your clothes looked like that mattered, it was who made them. This is something that totally baffles a lot of parents, and even if they're prepared to indulge your tastes for designer stuff, they can never understand what makes the things you want "better" than the cheap generic or chain-store versions, even when the things you want genuinely are slightly better designed, more stylish, marginally nicer. Parents tend to harp on a great deal about things being functional. They think that it doesn't matter who made them and even less whether anyone else is wearing or not wearing them. This might give you the impression that they simply don't understand the concept of fashion and style. Actually they *do* understand the concept very well when it's applied to things that matter to them, but they seem not to be able to apply it to anything else. Shame really.

There's not much point in arguing with your parents and trying to get them to see sense. The basic deal is that unless they are multi-millionaires they are probably permanently strapped for cash and wary that if they buy you something simply because it's fashionable, it might go out of fashion and you'll be back pronto asking them to buy you the next fashionable thing. As far as they're concerned, if they buy you something revolting and unfashionable, at least it will remain revolting and unfashionable, and therefore you'll hate it no more next month than you did when you first got it. But all this paints a bleak picture of parents. To be fair, they probably just want you to be happy, and do - at least some of the time - buy you the things you want just for the sheer joy of seeing your little face light up. The problem is that your parents do have a point - there *will*

always be something else that you desperately want just as much as the last thing you desperately wanted. It's a tough old world when you don't have unlimited amounts of cash, isn't it? Apart from declaring yourself a fashion-free zone, there are ways of coping in the consumer jungle.

Five Fascinating Facts For The Follower Of Fashion

★ If something comes into fashion, it's never worth pestering for it or breaking your piggy bank right away unless you truly adore it and could imagine yourself wearing it even *after* it went out of fashion. Wait a few weeks, and if you still want it, then it's probably worth it.

★ Never be afraid to avoid a fad you're not that crazy about, even if all your friends are doing it. Real friends don't care what you wear.

★ If there's no chance of getting anything new for a while, but you feel like your togs are hideously out of date, your best bet is to wear stuff that's either classic (like jeans and a sweatshirt) or totally off-beat, because it makes a positive statement that you're *aware* of fashion but have deliberately chosen not to follow it.

★ If there's a whole "look" that everyone's going for, you shouldn't immediately assume that you need to buy new stuff from head to toe - look carefully at what's being worn and you'll find that there's always one key item. Get hold of this, and you can team it with stuff you've already got , to capture the general look. This keeps you up-to-date whilst saving you money.

★ Don't get too hung up about fashion - there really are far more important things in life. If your friends disagree with this statement, it's worth seriously considering getting some new, less shallow ones.

SPOTS

When it comes to worries about appearance, spots are at the top of nearly everybody's list. Here are the facts:

★ Technically speaking, spots happen when a pore (one of the squillions of tiny little holes in your face that allow your skin to "breathe") gets blocked up with the skin's natural oil and the space underneath gets infected.

★ Teenagers and adolescents are more prone to spots because your skin starts producing more of its own oils, which can lead to blocked pores.

★ It's widely believed that not washing your face often enough or eating a lot of chocolate or oily, fried food increases the chances of this happening, but research shows that this is not necessarily the case. There's little proof that what you eat or do to your face makes any difference, although people who eat a super-healthy diet do usually seem to have good skin!

★ If you're prone to getting spots where your hair touches your face, it's probably because sweat and oils aren't getting a chance to escape. Try wearing your hair brushed back for a while.

★ Touching your face with your hands can encourage and spread spots, so avoid doing it.

★ Lots of spot preparations are very good, and well worth trying. There are different strengths available, but it's not always wise to go for the strongest - especially if you've got sensitive skin.

★ There's a product called Physoderm that you can buy from chemists to wash your face with, that is scientifically designed to control what your skin gets up to, and won't irritate your skin into producing more oil, even if you use it every day. Many people have found that it works wonders.

★ Acne is not the same as spots - it's a skin condition where you have a lot of large spots, either all over your face, or concentrated in one area. If you think you might have acne, it's worth visiting your doctor, who can check and provide you with the right stuff to sort it out, if necessary.

★ Picking or squeezing your spots is fun, but can definitely make them worse. If you must do it, wash your hands well before and afterwards.

★ Girls: covering spots with heavy layers of make-up can make them worse. If you want to hide them, try a medicated cover-stick instead.

★ The important thing to remember about spots above all else, is that almost everyone suffers from them, and although they may look horrendous to you, other people probably don't notice them half as much, if at all.

SKIN AND HAIR CARE - THE TRUTH

Adverts would have us believe that without this, that and the other brand - new, laboratory-tested, revolutionary, all-singing, all-dancing product, we will all be a bunch of lank-haired, spotty-faced, smelly and terminally unpopular human beings. It takes only a small segment of brain to work out for yourself that this is actually a load of old plop - we can all get by quite well, thank you, with just a few staple items that have been around forever. Even with this basic knowledge, though, we still get lured in by adverts because few of us can resist the chance that we could buy a little piece of magic - some fantastic potion which will give us that extra advantage. Although it's illegal to claim that a product does something that it can't, most ads still manage to be a bit of a con. In shampoo adverts, for instance, we see "before" and "after" shots of people with ordinary-bordering-on-dodgy hair ending up with shiny, bright, swingy hair. Most of us would naturally assume that it was the shampoo in question that had caused this transformation, but what the ad fails to reveal is the fact that the people's hair suddenly looks nice because it's been styled by a professional hairdresser. Oh well.

Even if you try to ignore the hype, buying grooming products is a tricky business. There are so many different products available and so much semi-scientific jargon written all over the bottles, pots and boxes that a trip to the chemist's can swiftly get as confusing as your average physics lesson. So what does it all mean? And do you actually need all this stuff? Read on for all you'll ever need to know about grooming products...

What The Heck *Is* This Stuff?
A Guide To Deciphering All That Jargon ...

★ "Two-in-one" shampoos
Shampoos that condition your hair as well as clean it.

★ Shampoos which "remove residue"
Shampoos that remove all the gunk that gets left on
your hair from other hair products (like styling aids and
other shampoos and conditioners) and can make it look
a bit lifeless. You don't need to use this kind of shampoo
all the time.

★ "Leave-in" conditioners
 Hair conditioners in cream or spray form which you
don't rinse out. They do the same job as regular
conditioners.

★ "Intensive conditioning treatments" and "Hair
treatment wax"
Often sachets or little individual tubes of conditioning
goo that you leave on your hair for quite a while before
rinsing. They're good for hair that is very dry or has
been damaged by perming or being dyed.

★ "Wet-look" gels
Unlike mousse, gel or styling lotions, these hairstyling
products are visible even when they dry. This is fine if

you're doing a hairstyle where you're slicking your hair back and want it to look neat and shiny. For any other hairstyle, choose another product!

★ "Modelling wax"
Heavy creams that, like "wet-look" gels, are best for slicking hair into place. They aren't so good on long hair (they can make it look greasy) but they're great for short styles.

★ "Foaming washes"
Gels and lotions you use with water to wash your face. They're like liquid soap for your face, and they don't dry your skin out.

★ "Toners"
Liquids you wipe onto your skin with cotton wool, which claim to close your pores and tighten up your skin and all that sort of thing. Some are also "astringent" which means that they clean your skin a bit and make it feel tingly.

★ Facial "masks"
Clay-based preparations that you leave to dry on your face, then rinse off. A "cleansing" mask will leave your face looking healthy and glowing - at least temporarily - although they can also dry your skin out. Moisturising masks work the same way but don't dry your skin out.

★ Facial "scrubs"
Creams or gels with little gritty bits in them that you rub on your face. They work by scraping off the dead skin cells, which makes your face look and feel "fresh".

★ "Buffers"
Little scratchy pads that you use to scrub your face. They work the same way as scrubs.

★ "Loofahs"
These are larger, for scrubbing your whole body rather than your face. Traditional loofahs look like big, scratchy, fat sticks, but you can get modern ones which consist of an abrasive pad on a long plastic handle (so that you can reach your back!).

Help! Which One Do I Buy?

Hair and face products are usually marked as being suitable for different types. But how do you know what type of hair or skin you have? Just read the descriptions and judge which sounds most like you ...

Hair
★ Dry hair
Never gets greasy, tends to get split ends and can go

frizzy, matted or "flyaway" pretty easily. If your hair is bleached, dyed with permanent colour, permed or straightened (in other words, it's been treated with chemicals) then it's probably dry (for now, anyway).

★ Normal hair
Looks healthy and shiny but not greasy. May get greasy at the roots if you don't wash it for a while, but otherwise pretty much behaves itself.

★ Greasy or oily hair
Just what it sounds like, although it doesn't necessarily mean that it's greasy all the time - just that it gets greasy quite quickly between washes.

★ Fine or flyaway hair
Thin, "baby-soft" hair that never behaves how you want it to.

Skin

★ Greasy or oily skin
Looks a bit shiny all over. Prone to spots all over (including on the cheeks).

★ Normal or combination skin
Dryish and soft on the cheeks, but sometimes a bit

shiny on the nose, forehead and chin, and prone to spots in those places, too. If you don't really have any trouble with your skin at all, then that's obviously normal skin too.

★ Dry skin
Dry all over, sometimes or all the time, can get patchy or flaky, sometimes feels "tight" or itchy.

★ Sensitive skin
Often gets flaky, patchy, itchy or blotchy. Goes red or bumpy when you use certain products.

Some True And Fascinating Facts About Grooming Products

★ Apart from dandruff shampoos and conditioning shampoos, a shampoo only does one job: cleans your hair. Mysterious claims like "energising" and "volumising" are largely guff.

★ Many shampoos are made specially for different types of hair - dry, normal or greasy. When a shampoo says it's "specially formulated" for your hair type there's no mystery to it - it just means that the detergent (cleaning) agent in the shampoo is stronger or weaker depending.

★ Very few people need to wash their hair every day, and too-frequent washing can make hair greasier because stimulating your scalp (which washing does) causes it to produce oil.

★ When choosing a conditioner, ignore any claims about "penetrating the hair shaft with vitamins" - this is pretty much impossible. Conditioners make your hair feel soft and look shiny by coating your hair with a kind of moisturiser.

★ You may well not need conditioner at all, especially if your hair is greasy or even just normal. If you find your hair gets lanky and lifeless when you use conditioner, the chances are that your hair doesn't need it.

★ Products which say that they can "mend" or get rid of split ends sound tempting, but it's actually impossible to stick hairs that have split back together. These products work in much the same way as conditioners - by smoothing down the surface of the hair and making it look less ratty. The only way to get rid of split ends is to cut them off!

★ Despite what the adverts might suggest, if you apply a styling product to your hair and just leave it, absolutely nothing will happen. Styling products are only as effective as what you do after you've put them on. The general idea is that you apply the gunk to your hair while it's damp then style it how you like it (by blow-drying, setting or just combing it into shape), and the styling product makes your hair stay roughly how you left it.

★ Nobody really needs hair styling products any more than people need to wear make up or jewellery. They can't change the way your hair is, just the way it looks, temporarily. If you're happy with the way your hair looks and how it behaves throughout the day, then you don't need styling products at all.

★ Any household soap will clean your face as effectively anything else you can buy. The only drawback is that soap can dry your skin out. This is something best avoided because it not only feels a bit tight and uncomfortable, but it can make your skin go flaky and patchy too. Cleansing bars look just like soap and work just like soap, but are designed not to dry your skin out, so they're a pretty good invention.

★ Unless you wear full make - up (foundation) every day, buying a cleansing cream to clean your face with is pointless.

★ Having a clean face is a nice feeling, but experts still disagree as to whether cleaning your face actually prevents spots (which, let's face it, is everybody's main aim). Some even say that frequently fiddling with your skin irritates it, makes it create extra oil and *causes* spots!

★ I personally feel that toners are a totally unnecessary product. A splash of cool water will do much the same job and although it doesn't look or smell as nice, it's a darn sight cheaper.

★ Moisturisers are creams, lotions and gels that make your skin feel smooth - end of story. Take no notice of blurb on products that claim to "penetrate the skin with active liposomes" or other such quasi-scientific mumbo-jumbo. Moisturisers basically work by adding moisture to the surface of your skin and preventing your skin from losing its own moisture.

★ Regardless of your sex, moisturiser is one product that almost everyone could do with, especially if you clean your face with soap and water. Even if you can't be bothered to use a moisturiser every day, it's worth using some occasionally, when your skin feels dry.

★ You don't need to spend a lot of money on a moisturiser. Experts agree that even the cheapest brands will do much the same job as the posh stuff you can buy for a 100 quid at department stores. Even something as simple as Vaseline or babies' nappy cream will work!

★ No one actually *needs* to use products like facial scrubs, because your skin is perfectly able to get rid of dead skin cells by itself. They're only worth the money if you love having that extra-clean feeling.

★ Even if you have bags under your eyes, it's not worth spending your money on commercial eye gels. Your bags are either genetic (i.e. a permanent part of your face) or caused by tiredness (in which case they're only temporary and will go away by themselves).

★ Lip lotions (like Blisteeze) are very effective for treating cold sores. However, it's virtually impossible to prevent them if you suffer from them, because they're caused by an internal virus that stays in your body.

SHOULD WE JUST LEAVE OUR SKIN ALONE?

There are many eminent dermatologists (medically-qualified skin specialists) in America who believe that the less you do to your skin the better. They say that the skin is capable of maintaining perfect condition by itself, and is irritated and damaged by all the fiddling that we subject it to. One of these boffins was recently quoted as saying that the fuss people make over their skin is bizarre, because it's just another of your body's organs, and the only difference between your skin and, say, your liver is that your skin is accessible. He says that he shudders to think what people might do if their liver was accessible - would we all spend hours scrubbing, cleaning and slathering it with creams? Would the chemists' shelves be over flowing with hundreds of products that claimed to keep our liver in tip-top condition? And would we buy them, even if we knew that our liver was able to maintain itself without our help? It's certainly interesting stuff to think about.

Chapter Nine

LEISURE

SCHOOL'S OUT!

What comes to mind when you think about the school holidays? Freedom? Fun? Frivolity? Or getting so bored that you feel you might be in danger of gnawing your own foot off if you have to stare at your bedroom wall for one more minute? Lovely as it is to have time off from the pressures of school, everyone feels bored in the holidays at some point. Parents aren't much help at suggesting things to combat your boredom - in fact, you may have noticed that the immortal words "I'm bored" seem to send them into a rage more befitting a comment like "Guess what, I've just run Granny over with the lawn mower!" Parents get annoyed when you're bored simply because they used to get bored in school holidays too, only now this horrible fact has dawned on them too late: the school holidays are just about the longest period of leisure time you get all in one go until you retire (and retirement doesn't really count because by then all your friends are really old and boring and will only want to do stupid things like play bridge and eat Danish pastries all the time) so you've got to make the most of it. It might be too late for your parents, but it's not too late for you. Next time you're bored in the hols, just consult my list of 50-50! - fabulously exciting things to try. Get reading, get off your backside, and get yourself a piece of the holiday action ... Or else shall we just make a date for a game of bridge some time around the year 2050? (The Danish pastries are on me.)

50 THINGS TO DO IN THE SCHOOL HOLIDAYS

Things To Do On Your Own

★ Rifle through your record collection and make compilation tapes. You could do one for yourself of all your all-time favourite tracks, create the ultimate tape for a party, or make one to give to your best friend as a pressie?

★ Organise a one-man fund raising event for your favourite charity, like a sponsored swim, walk or silence.

★ Load a camera with black and white film, then go out

and take some arty pictures of anything that takes your fancy (trees, buildings and old people are always particularly interesting).

★ Go through all your old family photos and pick out some interesting ones of yourself at various ages. Stick them onto sheets of paper, write your memories underneath them, staple the sheets together and hey presto - a pictorial history of your life that'll be brilliant fun to look back on.

★ Paint a picture then buy a cheap clip-on frame for it, and hang it on your wall.

★ Paint or draw a portrait of your favourite pop, TV or sports star and send it to them as a present (via their record or TV company or appropriate sports HQ).

★ Ask your parents if you can cook dinner one night. Reading through recipes, planning your menu and shopping for ingredients is just as much fun as the actual cooking.

★ Write a long, newsy letter to an old friend you haven't seen for ages, someone you went to nursery school with and haven't seen since, a neighbour from an area you left or perhaps to a distant relative in another country that you might not have even met.

★ Write your best friend a letter - even if you see them loads, they'll be really chuffed to get a letter, and getting a letter back from them in return will brighten up your morning.

★ Write off to a pen-friend organisation and get ready to get scribbling!

★ Make a "time capsule" - fill an air-tight tin (like a biscuit tin) with lots of things that you feel represent the year you live in (such as a picture from a fashion magazine, an instruction booklet from a computer game, the latest chocolate bar, a record sleeve from a recent single, a newspaper or anything else let your imagination run wild). Add a picture of yourself and a note saying who you are and what date you made the time capsule, then close the tin, wrap it in a plastic bag or polythene, Sellotaped tightly to make it waterproof and bury it deep in your garden (if you haven't got a garden, why not ask a friend or relative). The point is that one day someone will dig it up and be able to learn all about the '90s from *your* point of view. You could even dig it up yourself - as long as you promise to wait at least ten years!

★ Spend a day finding as many competitions as you can (look at magazines, food and other product packages and leaflets in your local shops), then enter them all - you might get lucky!

★ If you've got homework to do, why not try and do all of it in one day? Okay, it doesn't sound like much fun (probably because it isn't), but the immense feeling of pleasure, relaxation and relief you'll feel for the rest of the holidays is *well* worth one day of torture.

★ Re-arrange all the furniture in your bedroom, or start planning a full re decorating overhaul using our guide back in Chapter Six.

★ Go through your wardrobe and sort out all your clothes - finding things you'd forgotten about is almost as good as getting new stuff !

★ Plan your ideal birthday party down to the last detail - it's fun to plan even if you can't make it a reality for a while. Check out our party section, coming up next, for ideas.

★ Write a letter to the author of your favourite book (send it via their publishers) telling them how much you enjoyed reading it. Unlike pop, TV and movie stars, they always read their letters themselves and often write back.

★ Write off for information on what you can do to helpyour favourite charity, such as Greenpeace, the Anti-Vivisection League or Amnesty International.

★ If you live in an old house it can be fascinating to try and find out all about when it was built and who lived in it before you. Try your local town hall and library for info. Otherwise, why not find out about the history of your town, village or district instead.

★ Write a letter to yourself to be read when you're 18. Write about how you feel, the things that are important to you and how you hope your life will be when you're 18. Put it in an envelope marked with the date of your eighteenth birthday and keep it somewhere safe.

★ Try and make up a song. If it's any good, tape - record yourself singing it (or playing it, if you play an instrument) on cassette for posterity.

★ Draw a cartoon strip starring you and your family. Write an exaggerated version of your daily life, something funny that's happened to you all (what about a disastrous holiday?), or just make a story up.

Places To Visit

★ Go to the library and pick out some books that you'd never buy. That way you might discover something new and great, but as it's free, it doesn't matter if you decide not to read them.

★ Visit a museum or art gallery you've never been to before - I can promise that it won't be as dull as you might imagine.

★ Go and see an elderly relative or neighbour for a cup of tea and a chat - it'll make their day, and older people tend to have loads of fascinating stories to tell if you give them a chance (try asking about when they were young).

Things To Do With Your Parents

★ Ask your parents to dig out photos - or better still, home movies - of themselves when they were young. Then just sit back and marvel at how young they looked and what silly clothes they wore!

★ Ask your mum or dad if you can help out in their place of work for a day - it might just be interesting, and it certainly beats hanging round the house.

★ Ask your mum, dad or any older relative or family friend with some spare time on their hands if they can think of something they know how to do that you don't. Then ask them if they would be prepared to teach you how to do it. It could be anything - playing a game like chess or mah-jong, cooking something elaborate, painting with oil paints, fishing, French-plaiting hair, working a sewing machine or fixing a car engine. Even if it's something you didn't think you'd be interested in, you'll feel a huge sense of pride to end the holidays knowing more than you did at the start.

Things To Do With A Video Camera

★ If your family don't have a video camera, why not see if a relative will lend you theirs for a day, or else look into renting one from a video shop?

★ Make your own feature-film starring your friends and family, or just yourself - you never know, you could be the next Steven Spielberg!

★ Get together with one or more friends, dress up as a pop group or characters from a TV show or film, then film yourselves miming to a record or re-enacting a favourite scene!

★ Set up some pretend "home video bloopers", i.e. you and your friends and family "accidentally" falling into apaddling pool or opening a door onto someone who's carrying a cake! Try a few, then watch them back, pick the funniest one, and send it off to Jeremy Beadle in the hopes of winning some cash! Please don't try anything dangerous, though, or anything mean like making your baby brother eat a lemon!

Things To Do With Your Friends

★ Gather together two or more friends to plan and perform a show, dance display or play. You could just do it for fun in a day, or stretch out rehearsals over the summer, make it really good and perform for all your parents and pals or maybe even a local old people's home.

★ Organise a picnic where everyone brings something to eat (first discuss what everyone's going to bring). Eat it in the local park or in someone's garden, but don't be put off by dodgy weather - it's still fun even if you end up eating it under a tree or in the living - room!

★ Plan a day out where you and your friends each bring a little kid (a brother, sister, cousin or neighbour) and give them a treat like a visit to the zoo, cinema or local playground. I bet you'll enjoy it more than you'd imagine, and it'll earn you brownie points from parents neighbours, aunties etc. into the bargain.

★ Make your own photo-story. First make up a story and carefully plan a story-board for how each picture should look. Then go out and spend a day taking all the pictures. Once they've been developed, the fun really starts: glue them onto card or paper, and add all your speech bubbles and captions. Then see if you can use a photocopier at Mum or Dad's office (or else try a local printer's or the library) to run off some copies to share around with your friends and family. If it's really good, you could even try and sell copies when you're back at school!

★ Have a swap-shop at your house. Invite as many people as you can to come along and bring a certain number of things they don't want any more. Clothes, books, computer games, records, tapes and CDs are the best bet, and between five and ten items is ideal. When everyone's arrived, lay everything out neatly, then get grabbing. Everyone should take home the same number of things as they brought.

★ Have an all-day film festival: invite some pals round, pool your money, then rent three videos and stock up on popcorn. Try choosing the films around a theme, like a particular actor, director or genre. Some suggestions: films starring Macaulay Culkin (*Uncle Buck, Home Alone Home Alone II*); films directed by John Hughes ,

(*The Breakfast Club, Pretty In Pink, Ferris Buellers Day Off*); spooky films (*Beetlejuice, The Addams Family, Ghostbusters*); musicals (*Grease, West Side Story, Little Shop Of Horrors*).

★ Have an alternative film festival - each of you has to bring a movie that none of you has seen before (check up who's seen what over the phone beforehand).

★ Go to the library with a handful of friends and each pick out a book of short ghost stories. Spend the afternoon each flicking through your books to find the scariest and best story in each, then wait for it to get dark. Now turn off the lights, light a candle, huddle together and take it in turns to read out the stories you've chosen.

★ If there are four or more of you together, try this: get one sheet of paper and one pencil per person, and write each person's name at the top of each sheet. Now write the following headings on each sheet: best point, worst point, bad habits, biggest talent, brain-power, looks, dress sense and most suitable career. Write four on either side of the paper and leave a good - sized space underneath each heading. When you've done this, sit in a circle with your backs to the middle so no one can see what anyone else is writing and pass round the sheets,

making sure that no one has their own. Now everyone
has to write candid comments under each heading about
the person whose name is on the sheet they're holding.
You should all write in capital letters to disguise your
handwriting. When you've all done that, pass the sheets
around (making sure again that no one gets their own)
and repeat, until everyone has written comments about
everyone else. Finally, give everyone their own sheets to
read. It should be hard to tell who wrote what, so there
shouldn't be any fights. It's best when you're honest but
not too mean!

★ Get a friend (or two) and a cassette player and
pretend to be DJs on your own radio station. You could
just play your records and talk, but you could also make
up horoscopes, competitions and jingles. At the very
least you'll have a laugh doing it, and if it's brilliant,
you could even send it to your favourite local radio
station and ask for a summer job!

★ If you and your friends are into computer games,
why not organise a grand tournament? Pool together all
your best games and set rules for challenges (like
making it through a first level in the shortest time, or
scoring the most points within one minute). The winner
in each round gets one point (don't forget to keep
track!) and the grand champion is the person with the
most points when you run out of games.

★ If you're not into computers, you could have a tournament with board games - ask everyone to bring one or two with them, if you don't have enough at your house.

★ If your room needs redecorating and your parents give the okay, why not have a "painting party"? Ask a couple of friends round, get yourself a pot or two of paint and some brushes and transform your walls!

★ Test your psychic abilities! Find out if you or a friend are psychic by sitting in different rooms and having one of you think of a shape, word, colour or object, and the other try to draw or write down what they think the other is thinking. Take it in turns to be the "sender" or the "receiver".

★ If you and a friend are in a silly mood, why not dare each other to dress up really stupidly and walk to the shops. If you don't have any dressing-up clothes left from when you were a kid, you can always try wearing your own clothes backwards or putting a pair of pants on your head - highly goofy, but a good laugh, nevertheless!

★ If you have access to a tent, sleeping bags, torches and a garden, it can be brilliant fun to pitch up and spend the night outdoors. Ask your parents if you can eat dinner in there, then spend the night munching, chatting and telling spooky stories. If you can't find a real tent and it's not raining, you could always knock up a makeshift one using sheets, brooms, washing lines and anything else suitable.

★ Agree with a friend who you won't be able to see much during the holidays that you'll both write exciting diaries for the other to read. Make sure you write a little bit every day.

★ Set up your own "Green Team" - arrange to get together with some friends once a week and visit all your neighbours to ask if you can take their recyclable waste (like newspapers and bottles) to the nearest bottle bank or recycling centre for them.

★ Go to the local swimming baths in a big group and do something interesting like have a competition to see who can swim the most lengths, or invent your own synchronised swimming routine!

PARTY TIME!

A party is a funny old thing. It can be the most wonderful, unbelievable fun and something you'll remember forever, or the most horrendous nightmare (also guaranteed to stick permanently in your memory, unfortunately!). When the party is your own, it can be even more wonderful, or even more terrible.

A party needn't be complicated or expensive to be fun - you just need the right people, the right mood and a few tricks up your sleeve. The key to a successful party is careful forward planning, where you take *everything* into account and leaving nothing to chance. You don't need to wait until your birthday to throw a party, either - any excuse will do. If it's finances that are stopping you, why not see if you can split the cost with some friends and have a joint party, or persuade your parents that you'll fore go a birthday bash for this one (because they're bound to do something nice for you on your birthday anyway, like take you to dinner). If it's lack of ideas or fear of failure stopping you, then look no further than our definitive party guide...

Key

Very little planning and preparation

A bit of planning and preparation

A lot of planning and preparation

Cheap

Reasonably cheap

Fairly expensive

Expensive

Very little effort on the night

A bit of effort and organisation
needed on the night

A lot of effort and
organisation
needed on the night

Sleepover Party	"Proper" Party	Fancy Dress
The Basics		
Have a small group of friends round to stay the night, chat and eat snacky food.	Loads of friends, music, a darkened room, dancing, food, drink - the works!	The same as a "proper" party only with fancy dress and maybe a theme
Preparation		
Cost		
Effort on the night		
Plus points		
Easy, cheap, fun, and relaxed. Not much can go wrong	Exciting, feels like a real "event". A good excuse to get dressed up, which is always nice	Fun, memorable and guaranteed to get rid of inhibitions and get everyone in the party mood

Hazards

If there's a row, you're all stuck with each other for the entire night

People failing to be in the party spirit and just standing around, bored. Or, things getting wildly out of hand

People turning up in normal clothes, making everyone else feel silly and spoiling the atmosphere

Precautions

Ask only people that you know get along, and diffuse arguments before they start. Keep everyone occupied

Work hard to get everyone in the party mood. Make sure everyone's having a good time. Don't invite anyone you might not be able to control!

Keep a stash of suitably silly accessories or even a spare costume and force anyone in normal clothes to wear them !

The Key to Success

Keep a few things reserve in case you all get bored of just hanging out. A movie on video, computer and board games are ideal

Organise plenty of really great music ahead of time and work hard on making everyone dance - you might have to do this by setting an example!

Make sure that in everyone knows fancy dress is compulsory! Sort out some good music games ahead of time (making tapes is your best bet)

THIRTEENSOMETHING

Ice/Roller Skating	Bowling Party	Outdoor Party	Movie and Snack Party
The Basics			
Take a largish bunch of pals for a trip to the local ice or roller rink	Take a medium sized gang to a bowling alley for a few games and a snack	Invite a load of mates for a day of fun, food and frolics in your garden	Have a big group visit to the cinema followed by a bite to eat at a fast food place
Preparation			
Cost £			
Effort on Night			
Plus Points			
A good time is pretty much guaranteed. No effort once you've got everyone in	Good fun and not much effort once the teams are sorted out. Time to chat as well as play	You can lark about without fear of breaking stuff. Even just chatting is more fun outdoors	The entertainment is sorted, so there's no chance of people getting bored

Hazards

Adults on skates have a nasty habit of breaking limbs, resulting in dull trips to hospital

People taking the game too seriously, or not seriously enough, spoils it for everyone

Bad weather. Lack of things to do once the food's been eaten

Shuttling everyone to and from the cinema and snack bar can be dull and difficult to organise

Precautions

Try to persuade all but the most athletic adults to stay off the rink!

Keep a healthy spirit of competition going whilst keeping an eye out for anyone getting too worked-up !

Attempt only in summer and get distractions ready music, a football or even just a camera to take some silly pictures with

Keep the group quite small and plan ahead how you're going to get from one place to another (ideally, see if you can rope in adults with cars!)

The Key to Success

Buy a group-pass in advance to avoid hassle when you arrive. Pick a rink with a snack bar so you can hang out after skating

Book a lane in advance to avoid disaster. Choose teams in advance to avoid endless fannying about when you arrive

Good weather (impossible to guarantee unfortunately!). Plenty of stuff to do if everyone gets bored of just chatting

Pick a really great movie that everyone will like and a fast food place with plenty of room for you to sit around and hang out

Ten Highly Helpful Hints For Any Party

★ Obviously you're going to fix the facts about the date, basic details, number of people you want to invite and the overall cost with your parents, but it's a good idea to discuss everything else with them ahead of time too. There's nothing worse than having a row with your parents in front of all your mates because they've decided it's time the party was over, you don't want to stop yet and you haven't got a leg to stand on because you never agreed up front on how long the party would go on. It's also important for you and your parents to agree beforehand on what's allowed or not allowed (such as smoking) and where is out of bounds.

★ Invite everyone two or three weeks ahead, then double-check a week before to see if they can still come. You might even want to triple-check the day before, because there's nothing more miserable or disappointing than having a party where loads of people don't show up.

★ Write yourself a checklist of things you want to get and do so that you don't forget anything.

★ Don't just sort out the things you *know* you'll need, sort out stuff you *might* need as well (like a video to watch). If you don't use them, it doesn't matter, it's nice to know they're there.

★ Parties are usually more relaxed if your family isn't in the immediate vicinity, because *you'll* be more relaxed. Try to arrange for brothers and sisters to be out for the evening and for parents to keep their distance. It's nice for them to actually be in the house, though - first because you might need them for something, and second because knowing there are adults around keeps your guests',bad behaviour in check.

★ Being the host of a party can be a hugely daunting task - it's hard work, and you feel totally responsible if things don't turn out the way you planned. It's always worth considering appointing your best friend as co-host - two people can do the job more easily, you'll feel a lot less pressurised and it'll be fun to have someone to share all the excitement of getting everything prepared.

★ Think very carefully before you start inviting people. If you're only inviting a few people, take into consideration that some may not be able to come - you could end up with a pitiful turnout that'll make you miserable. Similarly, never ask more people than you reckon you can keep under control, or things could get horribly out of hand. Also make it clear if you don't want people to bring other people with them, or if you don't mind, find out exactly how many and who they are planning to bring so that you can keep the numbers in check.

★ Beware of gate-crashers if you're having a party at your house. Always have an adult or an older teenager on hand just in case, and always open the door yourself - if you let someone else do it (even your parents) they could assume that a gate-crasher is just a friend of yours they haven't met. Also, it's *always* wise to ask who's there before opening the door - not just at parties.

★ Keeping the music going is the key to a great party at home. Making tapes of your favourite tracks is the best bet, since you don't have those long, boring gaps while someone chooses what to put on next.

★ If you don't want to jeopardise your chances of being allowed to have another party, you've got to take total responsibility for everything, from your guests, behaviour to tidying up afterwards. Boring - yes, but you know it makes sense!

Chapter Ten

FRIENDS

Although your parents and family remain important to you all your life, your second decade on the planet is the one where you begin to make the break from them. Your parents' huge influence on you is gradually replaced by thinking more for yourself, and the other people you see from day to day at school become ever more important to you.

When you were at nursery, friendships were forged and destroyed in a matter of minutes. If someone called you a poo or stole your bag of crisps or some such thing, it was wildly upsetting for about ten seconds, then totally forgotten. At school, however, your friendships are far more intense to you, and hassle with your friends can seem like the end of the world.

When something is wrong in your friendships, it can seem like *everything* is wrong in your life. But no matter how bad things get, it's always all right in the end because no matter what happens to you in the years you're at school, you get a truly clean slate when you leave. You can see all the people you liked and avoid all the ones you didn't. You'll meet new people and have far more choice in who you spend your time with. Basically, you can start afresh. I know all this seems like little comfort if you're having trouble at school at the moment, because it's all quite a few years down the line, but it's useful to understand it now because it gives you a sense of perspective. By this I mean knowing that things which seem the be-all and end-all today will one day be just memories. If you're having problems with friendships at school, it can be helpful to know that there's always someone else who's been in a similar situation and come out the other side. It's easy for those people to look back on things and see what went wrong and how they could have worked things out better. Using someone else's hindsight can be very useful in tackling and understanding your own situation, so I talked to some adults about their school experiences...

"I OUTGREW HIM ..."

Everyone matures at a different rate, and when those rates are too different, friendships can crumble under the strain. Best friends Adam and John never imagined that it would happen to them, but it did. Adam remembers:

"The trouble began when we were about fourteen, and I started getting interested in girls. John still thought they were pretty boring, and couldn't understand it at all. I tried not to let it come between us, but the whole time he was treating me like I was mad to want to go out with with some girl when I could be knocking around with him, and he'd always get really upset when I went out on a date. I couldn't wait until he got interested in girls too, so he'd understand that you can go on dates *and* have a best friend, but it was too late: he got more and more stroppy and finally stopped speaking to me altogether. I met plenty of boys through the girls I was seeing, so I had mates to hang out with, but I missed John a lot."

John finally got a girlfriend a year or so later, but he still seemed to hold a grudge against Adam for "deserting" him. It was only when they ran into each other by chance, years after leaving school, that they became friends again. Looking back, Adam says:

"Even though John and I are friends again now, I still feel really sad about the old days. I think the problem was that we were both too embarrassed to talk about what was going on or how we felt. It's a shame that there's so much macho nonsense about boys not doing that sort of thing. If I had the chance over again, I'd definitely tell John how important our friendship was to me, and that seeing girls didn't change the way I felt about him. It'd be hard to say, but I'm sure it would have stopped the rift between us and saved us both a lot of misery."

"THREE'S A CROWD"

Debbie, Clare and Cathy were living proof that three friends could get on brilliantly without any trouble ... for a while, anyway. Debbie recalls:

"Everything was perfect until one summer holiday when I went away with my parents for four weeks. I really missed Clare and Cathy, but when I got back I found they'd seen each other nearly every day and they had all these little in-jokes. I felt totally left out. I thought the situation might improve back at school, but it got worse. They were still nice to me, but when we had to pair up in class, they made a beeline for each other, and they went to one another's houses after school most days and never invited me. It was a nightmare.
I didn't want to go to school and when I told my parents why, they didn't understand. Half the time I wished I was dead, the rest I wished that Clare and Cathy were."

Months later, Clare was off school for ages with flu and Debbie got a chance to change things.

"I got close to Cathy again. It was really nice to have one of my friends back properly, but I was pretty amazed that when Clare came back, Cathy tried to exclude her the way they'd excluded me. At first I was secretly enjoying the revenge, but I hated myself, because I knew how horrible it felt to be left out. I pulled myself together and tried really hard to get us all to be friends together again, the way it used to be, but it didn't work: there was always someone being left out. We'd lost all the trust and balance in our friendship."

Leaving school and making new friends was a huge relief for Debbie. She rarely speaks to Clare or Cathy, and says:

"I'll always feel quite fond of them, but I do resent the fact that I felt miserable such a lot of the time at school. I wish I'd had the courage to tell them both to bog off when they started getting stupid, and found some new friends right away, but I don't think I had it in me at the time."

"POPULARITY DOESN'T MEAN A THING!"

Nick wasn't just in with the in-crowd, he was it's leader, the most popular boy in his year. He never thought he'd have any problems, but he learnt that things don't always turn out the way you expect.

"I never gave my situation a lot of thought. I just knew that I had loads of friends, never had any trouble with girls and was always having a great time and I accepted it all as my lot in life."

When Nick left school to go to sixth form college, everything started to go wrong. He recalls:

"All my friends went off to different places or started jobs where they were hanging around with the people they worked with, and all of a sudden I was pretty much on my own. After having things so easy for so long, it was a horrible shock. I went to college with totally the wrong attitude: I just expected to resume my role as Mr. Popular automatically. Whilst I was sitting around waiting for people to flock to me, everyone else was making a proper effort to get to make friends and the result was that everyone thought I was totally arrogant. Eventually I got a couple of mates, but I was always painfully aware of other blokes being more popular than me, which I wasn't used to."

These days, Nick is a far quieter, more humble person than he was at school. He says:

"My story goes to show that no matter how school goes for you, what happens afterwards is totally up to you. I can't really complain: I'm lucky to have had such a great time at school, but it was quite a bad preparation for real life, as I never learnt to cope in situations where I didn't get my own way. I suppose people at my school who were unhappy and unpopular and envied me, might be comforted to know that I didn't always have it easy. I hope they wouldn't take too much glee in my misery though, because I couldn't help being popular and I never did them any harm."

"I JUST COULDN'T HELP PICKING ON HER ..."

Alison wasn't nasty by nature. So why did she make her friend Kate's life a misery?

"When I first met Kate, she was loud and confident and outgoing - a lot like me. We got along really well, and together with Chrissie, the prettiest girl in the class, we were a popular gang. The problem was that we were all such strong personalities that something had to give - and it did. We started ganging up on each other, almost as if we were testing each other's strength of character to see who was boss. Being the victim didn't bother me because I knew that I could be friends with other people if I got sick of it, and I always made that clear. Chrissie's reaction was similar, but Kate took it very badly and always got really hysterical. For some reason I found that very entertaining, and picked on Kate more and more. She very quickly went from being loud and confident to being a clingy, neurotic doormat. I was constantly working out new ways to upset her, and I guess Chrissie was too afraid that I'd turn on her to do anything but back me up. It always amazed me that Kate still wanted to be my friend, but in fact it seemed to make her even more keen. The strange thing is that I actually really liked her - I just enjoyed the big reaction I got from being nasty to her - it was fun for me."

Everything changed when Chrissie made some new friends and stopped hanging around with Alison and Kate. Alison remembers:

"Being mean to Kate without having anyone to share it with wasn't as much fun for me, so I was nice to her instead and we became best friends. Later she became friendly with a swotty girl called Caroline, and encouraged me to gang up on her. Looking back, she was probably trying to get what I'd done to her out of her system."

Although Kate moved abroad, she and Alison have stayed friends to this day. Says Alison:

"We get on really well now, although Kate still talks quite a lot about how nasty I was to her and I think she feels quite bitter. I don't feel remorse, though, because I really couldn't help it. I think it's human nature, especially when you're young, to do as much as you think you can get away with. If Kate had ever said to me "I like you, but I've had enough of you being mean, and unless you stop it I don't want to be friends any more," I'd have respected her a great deal for it and I'd probably have stopped. In the end it all comes down to self-respect: if you act like you don't care how people treat you, there will always be someone who'll go ahead and walk all over you."

"I DIDN'T WANT TO BE JUST HIS SIDE-KICK"

Paul and Alex had been best friends since they were little, but when they became part of a big gang at secondary school, everything changed.

" I didn't really like this group of boys, but Alex did and he was my best friend so I stuck by him, but the worst was yet to come. Alex got into bullying boys outside of our group, and soon everyone was scared of him. They were scared of me too, because I was his friend, which meant they left me alone, but I wasn't at all happy. I was going off Alex rapidly, I always felt sorry for the people he was bullying, and the more notorious he got, the more I was in his shadow. No one took any notice of me at all, and eventually Alex didn't either - he was more interested in scaring people and chatting up girls. I was miserable."

Six months later, Paul felt so sorry for a new boy whose money Alex had stolen that he secretly retrieved it from Alex's bag and gave it back.

"He was so pleased, and when we got chatting we found out we had loads in common. The next day I sat with him and hung around with him at break instead of Alex, and it was such a relief to just be quiet and normal again. Alex pretended not to mind, but then he turned up at my house that night crying and yelling that I was a wimp. After that he didn't speak to me any more, but he never gave me a hard time or anything."

These days Paul doesn't see anyone from school. He says:

"After I stopped being friends with Alex there were times when I really missed him - after all, we'd been friends for so long. I know now that I did the right

178

thing, though, because he wasn't going to change, and I
didn't want to be just his side-kick. My only regret is
that I didn't work that out earlier and that I spent so
long being miserable, but that's life. I was fine in the
end."

"WE WERE IN A LITTLE WORLD OF OUR OWN ..."

*Richard and Joe shared a love of comics and a great friendship.
Did it really matter if everyone else thought they were weird?
Richard recalls:*

"We never took any notice of anyone else - we were very
shy - but we were really happy, just collecting comics
and wishing we could be superheroes! The other kids
teased us at first, but we ignored them and they left us
alone. My parents were concerned that I only had one
friend, and never got involved in any school activities,
but my school work was fine, so they couldn't complain.
The only time I felt vaguely unhappy was when all the
other boys were having fun playing football, and we
were totally left out."

*Everything was fine until the other boys in the class got into
fashion. Says Richard:*

"The teasing started again because Joe and I both wore horrible hand-me-downs (we were clueless about fashion, and all our money went on comics anyway) and I started to feel more self-conscious about how different we were. I made an effort to blend in and take more notice of the other kids, and it was nice, because I found out that there was more to life than comics! Sadly it was all a bit too late - it was shortly before I left school!"

These days Richard and Joe are still friends, and still collect comics, but Richard isn't shy any more - he's loud, confident, successful and has lots and lots of friends. He says:

"I am living proof that you can't tell what someone is going to be like as an adult from the way they are at school! I sometimes feel a little envious when other people talk about all the great times they had at school, but I was very happy indeed in my own little world, and I'm quite proud that I always had the courage to be myself."

"I DESPERATELY WANTED TO JOIN THE IN-CROWD"

Sarah had five fun, loyal friends, but she wasn't happy: all she wanted was to be in with the gang everyone called "the Big Group". She explains:

"The Big Group were basically the 'in crowd', and it consisted of boys and girls, all much cooler and more grown-up than us, we thought. I think most of our year would have liked to join them, but they were definitely a closed shop. While the other girls were resigned to this, I was totally obsessive, and never got over wanting to join. I shared a lift to and from school with Miranda, one of the girls from the Big Group, which made me feel that somehow I was in with a better chance. Miranda and I got on really well out of school, but she could never understand why I'd want to dump my friends and go around with hers. I always thought that was easy for her to say when she was already part of the Big Group , but in retrospect, I think she was actually a lot more mature than me, and genuinely wouldn't care who she hung out with if she was happy."

After a row with her friends one day, Sarah spent break time with Miranda and the Big Group.

"It was nowhere near as much fun as I'd dreamed it would be, but when I returned to my friends the next day, the urge to join the Big Group was still as strong as ever - I was clinging onto my fantasy even though I'd seen the reality. I never stopped feeling discontented and I eventually declared school a write off, made some friends outside and decided that I would be happy only when I left."

THIRTEENSOMETHING

Sarah was indeed very happy after she left school, and is still happy now, despite it all. She says:

"Looking back I do wish that I'd been more contented with my lot and made more effort to enjoy school life because I'd probably have been happier, but making friends outside of school was a good solution for me, because it gave me a taste of the real world, and I'm still friends with most of those people now. The only person I'm still friendly with from school is Miranda.

I realise now how idiotic it was that I would have been prepared to drop my lovely friends for a bunch of people who were no more fun and probably less nice or genuine than my friends. In terms of my story having a moral, it should really end with me lonely and friendless to prove that you should never take people for granted, but those things only happen in books. Actually my school days have made no difference at all to the rest of my life. The only thing I've learnt from it all is that sadly, "fitting in" is a big deal at school, and I just didn't fit in - not with my friends, and not (I realise now) with the in-crowd either, who, apart from Miranda, were all pretty shallow. Even though I wasn't always happy back then, I can see now that it was all part of a very healthy, very important process. Choosing friends, making friends, dumping friends and losing friends is all part of finding out who you are - and that's what these days of your life are all about."